PAUL
AND ME

PAUL
AND ME

A Journey to and from the Damascus Road
From Islam to Christ

KARIM SHAMSI-BASHA

With Selections from
James Stalker, J. Gresham Machen & B.B. Warfield

Solid Ground Christian Books
Birmingham, Alabama USA

Solid Ground Christian Books
P.O. Box 660132
Vestavia Hills, Alabama 35266
(205) 443-0311
mike.sgcb@gmail.com
www.solid-ground-books.com

PAUL and me
A Journey to and from the Damascus Road
From Islam to Christ

Karim Shamsi-Basha

www.paulandme.com

Cover photograph by Karim Shamsi-Basha
All photographs in the book are Copyright Karim Shamsi-Basha - 2013
Photographs of Karim in therapy are Copyright Hal Yager

Cover design by Borgo Design
borgogirl@gmail.com

ISBN- 978-159925-291-9

Cover caption: *The Street Called Straight (Share' El Doughry) begins at the Eastern Gate in Damascus– Syria. The structure is the only original Roman gate still standing over the Christian quarter of the city. Dating back to 200 AD, the gate still reminds people of the street mentioned in the 9th chapter of the book of Acts. This is the same street Saint Paul was led to after the blinding light on the Road to Damascus, and the same one Ananias was told to go to and heal the Apostle. The House of Saint Ananias, where the healing took place, lies just inside the gate.*

DEDICATION

First of all I give my praise and thanksgiving to my Lord and Savior Jesus Christ for His guidance along this journey.

My deepest gratitude goes to my three children: Zade, Dury, and Demi; their love is what made this writing possible. My love also goes to my father, who passed away in 2005 a Muslim. He inspired me to "explore" religion at a young age, and to the rest of my family in Syria. I am also indebted to my publisher, Michael, for the countless hours and days he spent poring over the manuscript to insure its accuracy and flow – for writing the preface – and for choosing the material from Stalker, Warfield, and Machen. Thanks to Dick for introducing me to Michael, and for his precise editing. Also thank you to Easty Lambert-Brown for the wonderful cover design, and to Linda for the tireless copy-editing. I am also grateful to Brian for the wonderful website.

Now I get to thank the three very special people: Gil for starting me on the road to Christianity, Dana for leading me to true Salvation - and for inspiring the name of the book; and Frank for guiding my journey through teaching me the Word – and for writing the Foreword. My love and respect for them is immense. And I wish to also thank all those who have prayed for me and have supported me.

Finally I would like to thank the Lord for giving Hanrietta the boldness to do what had to be done.

*My family: father Kherridean, mother Laila, oldest sister Rowaida (left),
oldest brother Maher (right), sister Mimi (bottom right), and me (bottom left).*

TABLE OF CONTENTS

A LETTER TO MY FAMILY

I write you this letter to seek to explain to you the direction I have taken in my life. In your eyes, I fear you view me as a traitor who left his religion. A traitor who turned his back on Islam, the religion that I grew up in the midst of. The religion of my father and his father. The religion I was supposed to embrace and die holding to its principles. I am afraid this book will bring shame upon you. And it is entirely possible it may cause some to deny my existence or even disown me.

I want you to understand that I write this with all the love in my heart for you. The love of God is what saved me, and the love of God can save you as well. You don't have to be ashamed because I chose a different path. Just be at peace with the fact that this different path can actually lead to loving God instead of fearing Him. It can lead to God dwelling within you instead of being far from you. It can lead to a God who wants to commune and fellowship with you.

Please read this book with an open mind. Read it with the idea that it might be your way out of bondage. Do not count me dead just because I chose a different road and wrote about it. Consider me your son, brother, cousin, friend, and the one you loved once in the past. I love you with all of my heart. And I pray that the grace and love of God will light up your path towards Him.

I pray that peace will reign in Syria. As this book goes to print, the situation is becoming more complex as the Arab World hemorrhages. My prayers are with you who have to remain in a war-torn country.

May His mercy be with you, may His Salvation find you, and may His power protect you.

With love and with Christ,

مع الحب ومع المسيح

Karim

كريم

FOREWORD

Karim has drawn an interesting analogy of his spiritual journey and the Apostle Paul's. It is truly an intriguing parallel. Karim's near-death experiences and Paul's, the big shift required to believe in Christ, the struggle to accept the overwhelming implications of Christ's claims, the dramatic life-changing impact when Christ is truly accepted – all come through loud and clear.

A special feature of this book is the insertion of selections from two of my favorite authors, B. B. Warfield and J. Gresham Machen. I am glad that you will be introduced to men whose writings can truly change your life as they have mine.

This book is also very instructive concerning the barriers Muslims and those of other religions face in accepting the claims of the Gospel, and gives insight into how to help them work their way through these barriers. Karim has done a lot of research on the evidence of the truth of the Bible and brings out excellent material for a solid foundation for faith.

It has been my privilege to assist Karim in his amazing spiritual journey and to see the fruit being borne. I highly recommend this intriguing and instructive account.

Dr. Frank Barker
Pastor Emeritus
Briarwood Presbyterian Church
Birmingham, Alabama

PREFACE

Being a publisher for more than twenty years has been both rewarding and challenging. One of the challenges has been sifting and sorting through a multitude of books submitted to me for consideration. As soon as Karim Shamsi-Basha learned that I was a publisher he told me about two books he was writing. He asked if we could meet to discuss them. Somewhat reluctantly I agreed to do so. I thank the Lord that I did. From the first moment, I became convinced that Karim was a very special man, and his story was a very special story.

For several months we have met weekly and spent hours poring over his manuscript. As you will learn, his father was a gifted writer in Syria, and he appears to have passed that gift on to his youngest child. One thing that makes this book unique is that it tells the story of two very different lives, one who was born and raised in Damascus, and the other who was wondrously converted on the way to Damascus. These two lives intersect at many points, and we have constructed this book in a way that will allow you to see both of these lives for themselves.

Karim will tell his story in his own words. He asked me to tell the story of the Apostle Paul. Instead I have decided to allow Paul to tell his own story as set forth in the Bible, with added commentary by three gifted men from the past who greatly loved the great Apostle. James Stalker (1848-1927) was a Scottish minister who was best known for his preaching and his two workbooks on *The Life of Jesus Christ* and *The Life of Saint Paul*. We will draw several sections from this latter book as we set out Paul's life for you. Benjamin B. Warfield (1851-1921) was an American born biblical and theological scholar of the first rank. He is my favorite author outside the Bible and we will draw material from sermons and articles he wrote on the life and ministry of the Apostle. Finally, J. Gresham Machen (1881-1937) was also an American born biblical and theological scholar of the first rank, and a bold defender of the faith, who has written a great deal on Paul and his impact on the world. These men will unite their voices in setting forth the early life, the conversion and the ministry of one of the most important men to walk this earth.

You are about to begin a journey that has the potential of turning your world upside down, or better right side up. Take the time to read each chapter prayerfully and carefully. Each person who picks up this book will begin the journey in a different place. Some will begin with indifference about the God of the Bible, others perhaps with a prejudice against the God of the Bible for any number of reasons. Others will begin with a mind and heart persuaded that the God of the Bible is the one true God whom they love and seek to worship and serve. Whatever your case may be, it is our prayer and heart's desire that you will ask two questions, both in the form of prayer: First, "Show me myself." And second, "Show me Yourself." The knowledge of God and of ourselves is the sum of all saving knowledge. May this humble book be used to lead you to the wisdom that is from above.

Michael Gaydosh
Founder of Solid Ground Christian Books

PAULINE INTRODUCTION

Why Paul is the Model Christian
by James Stalker

The Man for the Time. There are some men whose lives it is impossible to study without receiving the impression that they were expressly sent into the world to do a work required by the juncture of history on which they fell. The story of the Reformation, for example, cannot be read by a devout mind without wonder at the providence by which such great men as Luther, Zwingli, Calvin and Knox were simultaneously raised up in different parts of Europe to break the yoke of the papacy and republish the gospel of grace.

This impression is produced by no life more than by that of the Apostle Paul. He was given to Christianity when it was in its most rudimentary beginnings. It was not, indeed, feeble, nor can any mortal man be spoken of as indispensable to it; for it contained within itself the vigor of a divine and immortal existence, which could not but have unfolded itself in the course of time. But, if we recognize that God makes use of means which commend themselves even to our eyes as suited to the ends He has in view, then we must say that the Christian movement at the moment when Paul appeared upon the stage was in the utmost need of a man of extraordinary endowments, who, becoming possessed with its genius, should incorporate it with the general history of the world; and in Paul it found the man it needed.

A Type of Christian Character. Christianity obtained in Paul an incomparable type of Christian character. It already, indeed, possessed the perfect model of human character in the person of its Founder, Jesus Christ. But He was not as other men, because from the beginning He had no sinful imperfection to struggle with; and Christianity still required to show what it could make of imperfect human nature. Paul supplied the opportunity of exhibiting this. He was naturally of immense mental stature and force. He would have been a remarkable man even if he had never become a Christian. The other apostles would have lived and died in the obscurity of Galilee if they had not been lifted into prominence by the Christian movement; but the name of Saul of Tarsus would have been remembered still in some character or other even if Christianity had never existed. Christianity got the opportunity in him of showing to the world the whole force it contained. Paul was aware of this himself, though he expressed it with perfect modesty, when he said, "For this cause I obtained mercy, that in me as chief might Jesus Christ show forth all His long-suffering for an example of them who should hereafter believe on Him to everlasting life."

His conversion proved the power of Christianity to overcome the strongest prejudices and to stamp its own type on a large nature by a revolution both instantaneous and permanent. Paul's was a personality so strong and original that no other man could have been less expected to sink himself in another; but, from the moment when he came into contact with Christ, he was so overmastered with His influence that he never afterward had any other desire than to be the mere echo and reflection of Him to the world.

But, if Christianity showed its strength in making so complete a conquest of Paul, it showed its worth no less in the kind of man it made of him when he had given himself up to its influence. It satisfied the needs of a peculiarly hungry nature, and never to the close of his life did he betray the slightest sense that this satisfaction was abating. His constitution was originally compounded of fine materials, but the spirit of Christ, passing into these, raised them to a pitch of excellence altogether unique.

Nor was it ever doubtful either to himself or to others that it was the influence of Christ which made him what he was. The truest motto for his life would be his own saying, "I live, yet not I, but Christ liveth in me." Indeed, so perfectly was Christ formed in him that we can now study Christ's character in his, and beginners may perhaps learn even more of Christ from studying Paul's life than from studying Christ's own. In Christ Himself there was a blending and softening of all the excellences which makes His greatness elude the glance of the beginner, just as the very perfection of Raphael's painting makes it disappointing to an untrained eye; whereas in Paul a few of the greatest elements of Christian character were exhibited with a decisiveness which no one can mistake, just as the most prominent characteristics of the painting of Rubens can be appreciated by every spectator.

A Great Thinker. Christianity obtained in Paul, secondly, a great thinker. This it specially needed at the moment. Christ had departed from the world, and those whom He had left to represent Him were unlettered fishermen and, for the most part, men of no intellectual mark. In one sense this fact reflects a peculiar glory on Christianity, for it shows that it did not owe its place as one of the great influences of the world to the abilities of its human representatives: not by might nor by power, but by the Spirit of God, was Christianity established in the earth. Yet, as we look back now, we can clearly see how essential it was that an apostle of a different stamp and training should arise.

Paul was a born thinker. His mind was of majestic breadth and force. It was restlessly busy, never able to leave any object with which it had to deal until it had pursued it back to its remotest causes and forward into all its consequences. It was not enough for him to know that Christ was the Son of God: he had to unfold this statement into its elements and understand precisely what it meant. It was not enough for him to believe that Christ died for sin: he had to go farther and inquire why it was necessary that He should do so and how His death took sin away.

But not only had he from nature this speculative gift: his talent was trained by education. The other apostles were unlettered men; but he enjoyed the fullest scholastic advantages of the period. In the rabbinical school he learned how to arrange and state and defend his ideas. We have the issue of all this in his Epistles, which contain the best explanation of Christianity possessed by the world. The right way to look at them is to regard them as the continuation of Christ's own teaching. They contain the thoughts which Christ carried away from the earth with him unuttered. Of course Jesus would have uttered them differently and far better. Paul's thoughts have everywhere the coloring of his own mental peculiarities. But the substance of them is what Christ's must have been if he had himself given them expression.

The Missionary of the Gentiles. Christianity obtained in Paul, thirdly, the missionary of the Gentiles. It is rare to find the highest speculative power united with great practical activity; but these were united in him. He was not only the Church's greatest thinker, but the very foremost worker she has ever possessed. We have been considering the speculative task which was awaiting him when he joined the Christian community; but there was a no less stupendous practical task awaiting him too. This was the evangelization of the Gentile world.

Originally attached more strictly than any of the other apostles to the peculiarities and prejudices of Jewish exclusiveness, he cut his way out of the jungle of these prepossessions, accepted the equality of all men in Christ, and applied this principle relentlessly in all its issues. He gave his heart to the Gentile mission, and the history of his life is the history of how true he was to his vocation. There was never such singleness of eye or wholeness of heart. There was never such superhuman and untiring energy. There was never such an accumulation of difficulties victoriously met and of sufferings cheerfully borne for any cause. In him Jesus Christ went forth to evangelize the world, making use of his hands and feet, his tongue and brain and heart, for doing the work which in His own bodily presence He had not been permitted by the limits of His mission to accomplish.

INTRODUCTION

Why I was Compelled to Write this Book

*My family and I had lunch in the mountains
North of Damascus during my visit in 2002.*

First things first: By writing this book, I am by no means comparing myself to the Apostle Paul, for he was able to say in 1 Corinthians 11:1, *"Be imitators of me, as I am of Christ."* This is what Adolphe Monod says in Saint Paul about the Apostle's admonition: "Try to imagine the most exemplary Christian you have even known saying to anyone, 'Imitate me' . . . It represents a holiness so great and yet so simple that it rises as far above the precautions of modesty as it does above the pretensions of self-love, so as to give glory to God's grace alone."

The Apostle Paul is one of the most influential people in the history of Christianity. I am a humble servant who happened to be born in the city of Damascus, where Paul had his conversion. Damascus is the oldest inhabited city on earth, draped in thousands of years' worth of ancient and historic vines. I walked the same roads and was around the Street Called Straight in my youth, not knowing it was where Paul retreated after the blinding light. To a young Muslim boy, it was just another street.

Paul converted to Christianity on the Road *to* Damascus; I converted on the Road *from* Damascus – two very different stories, two very different men - the same Salvation, and the same Lord and Savior. The parallels I draw are based on scripture and my story, a story of a smooth life interrupted by a near-death experience that left me yearning for purpose. Surviving an event that kills most people was a huge wake-up call, but it was not the only wake-up call. I had one even before I was born!

The glorious story of the Apostle Paul and my demure story intersect at several junctures, as you will soon see. I have been compelled to write by a burning desire to share the grace of God with people all over the world. I am confident that the Lord has graciously chosen to lead me step by step in His perfect will for my life, despite my failure to follow. I am also confident that He intends that my story be used to help others who are experiencing the darkness I once knew.

Enjoy the journey, and use the blank page at the end of each chapter to record your own journey. Many readers will find their own parallels with Paul's story. You don't have to be born in Damascus to experience God's abundant grace, and you don't have to travel to Damascus to revel in His ubiquitous Salvation. You can draw your own parallels to the journey of this extraordinary man. And as you do, remember that God sends us different wake-up calls, be it a blinding light or a brain aneurysm—we just have to recognize the call, and act upon it.

God's Preparation of the Apostle Paul
by James Stalker

God's Plan.—Persons whose conversion takes place after they are grown up are wont to look back upon the period of their life which has preceded this event with sorrow and shame and to wish that an obliterating hand might blot the record of it out of existence. St. Paul felt this sentiment strongly: to the end of his days he was haunted by the specters of his lost years, and was wont to say that he was the least of all the apostles, who was not worthy to be called an apostle, because he had persecuted the Church of God. But these somber sentiments are only partially justifiable. God's purposes are very deep, and even in those who know Him not He may be sowing seeds which will only ripen and bear fruit long after their godless career is over. Paul would never have been the man he became or have done the work he did, if he had not, in the years preceding his conversion, gone through a course of preparation designed to fit him for his subsequent career. He knew not what he was being prepared for; his own intentions about his future were different from God's; but there is a divinity which shapes our ends, and it was making him a polished shaft for God's quiver, though he knew it not.

The place of his birth was Tarsus, the capital of the province of Cilicia, in the southeast of Asia Minor. It stood a few miles from the coast, in the midst of a fertile plain, and was built upon both banks of the river Cydnus, which descended to it from the neighboring Taurus Mountains, on the snowy peaks of which the inhabitants of the town were wont, on summer evenings, to watch from the flat roofs of their houses the glow of the sunset. Not far above the town the river poured over the rocks in a vast cataract, but below this it became navigable, and within the town its banks were lined with wharves, on which was piled the merchandise of many countries, while sailors and merchants, dressed in the costumes and speaking the languages of different races, were constantly to be seen in the streets. The town enjoyed an extensive trade in timber, with which the province abounded, and in the long fine hair of the goats kept in thousands on the neighboring mountains, which was made into a coarse kind of cloth and manufactured into various articles, among which tents, such as Paul was afterward employed in sewing, formed an extensive article of merchandise all along the shores of the Mediterranean. Tarsus was also the center of a large transport trade; for behind the town a famous pass, called the Cilician Gates, led up through the mountains to the central countries of Asia Minor; and Tarsus was the depot to which the products of these countries were brought down, to be distributed over the East and the West.

The inhabitants of the city were numerous and wealthy. The majority of them were native Cilicians, but the wealthiest merchants were Greeks. The province was under the sway of the Romans, the signs of whose sovereignty could not be absent from the capital, although Tarsus itself enjoyed the privilege of self-government. The number and variety of the inhabitants were still further increased by the fact that, like the city of Glasgow, Tarsus was not only a center of commerce, but also a seat of learning. It was one of the three principal university cities of the period, the other two being Athens and Alexandria; and it was said to surpass its rivals in intellectual eminence. Students from many countries were to be seen in its streets, a sight which could not but awaken in youthful minds thoughts about the value and the aims of learning.

Who does not see how fit a place this was for the Apostle of the Gentiles to be born in? As he grew up, he was being unawares prepared to encounter men of every class and race, to sympathize with human nature in all its varieties, and to look with tolerance upon the most diverse habits and customs. In after life he was always a lover of cities. Whereas his Master avoided Jerusalem and loved to teach on the mountainside or the shore of the lake, Paul was constantly moving from one great city to another. Antioch, Ephesus, Athens, Corinth, Rome, the capitals of the ancient world, were the scenes of his activity. The words of Jesus are redolent of the country, and teem with pictures of its still beauty or homely toil—the lilies of the field, the sheep following the shepherd, the sower in the furrow, the fishermen drawing their nets; but the language of Paul is impregnated with the atmosphere of the city and alive with the tramp and hurry of the streets. His imagery is borrowed from scenes of human energy and monuments of cultivated life—the soldier in full armor, the athlete in the arena, the building of houses and temples, the triumphal procession of the victorious general. So lasting are the associations of the boy in the life of the man.

Education.—It is a question natural to ask, whether, before leaving home to go and get his training as a rabbi, Paul attended the University of Tarsus. Did he drink at the wells of wisdom which flow from Mount Helicon before going to sit by those which spring from Mount Zion? From the fact that he makes two or three quotations from the Greek poets it has been inferred that he was acquainted with the whole literature of Greece. But, on the other hand, it has been pointed out that his quotations are brief and commonplace, such as any man who spoke Greek would pick up and use occasionally; and the style and vocabulary of his Epistles are not those of the models of Greek literature, but of the Septuagint, the Greek version of the Hebrew Scriptures, which was then in universal use among the Jews of the Dispersion. Probably his father would have considered it sinful to allow his son to attend a heathen university. Yet it is not likely that he grew up in a great seat of learning without receiving any influence from the academic tone of the place. His speech at Athens shows that he was able, when he chose, to wield a style much more stately than that of his writings, and so keen a mind was not likely to remain in total ignorance of the great monuments of the language which he spoke.

There were other impressions, too, which the learned Tarsus probably made upon him: its university was famous for those petty disputes and rivalries which sometimes ruffle the calm of academical retreats; and it is possible that the murmur of these, with which the air was often filled, may have given the first impulse to that scorn for the tricks of the rhetorician and the windy disputations of the sophist which form so marked a feature in some of his writings. The glances of young eyes are clear and sure, and even as a boy he may have perceived how small may be the souls of men and how mean their lives, when their mouths are filled with the finest phraseology.

The college for the education of Jewish rabbis was in Jerusalem, and thither Paul was sent about the age of thirteen. His arrival in the Holy City may have happened in the same year in which Jesus, at the age of twelve, first visited it, and the overpowering emotions of the boy from Nazareth at the first sight of the capital of his race may be taken as an index of the unrecorded experience of the boy from Tarsus. To every Jewish child of a religious disposition Jerusalem was the center of all things; the footsteps of prophets and kings echoed in the streets; memories sacred and sublime clung to its walls and buildings; and it shone in the glamor of illimitable hopes.

It chanced that at this time the college of Jerusalem was presided over by one of the most noted teachers the Jews have ever possessed. This was Gamaliel, at whose feet Paul tells us he was brought up. He was called by his contemporaries the Beauty of the Law, and is still remembered among the Jews as the Great Rabbi. He was a man of lofty character and enlightened mind, a Pharisee strongly attached to the traditions of the fathers, yet not intolerant or hostile to Greek culture, as were some of the narrower Pharisees. The influence of such a man on an open mind like Paul's must have been very great; and, although for a time the pupil became an intolerant zealot, yet the master's example may have had something to do with the conquest he finally won over prejudice.

At Jerusalem.—We cannot tell in what year Paul's education at the college of Jerusalem was finished or where he went immediately afterward. The young rabbis, after completing their studies, scattered in the same way as our own divinity students do, and began practical work in different parts of the Jewish world. He may have gone back to his native Cilicia and held office in some synagogue there. At all events, he was for some years at a distance from Jerusalem and Palestine; for these were the very years in which fell the movement of John the Baptist and the ministry of Jesus, and it is certain that Paul could not have been in the vicinity without being involved in both of these movements either as a friend or as a foe.

But before long he returned to Jerusalem. It was as natural for the highest rabbinical talent to gravitate in those times to Jerusalem as it is for the highest literary and commercial talent to gravitate in our day to the metropolis. He arrived in the capital of Judaism very soon after the death of Jesus; and we can easily imagine the representations of that event and of the career thereby terminated which he would receive from his Pharisaic friends.

We have no reason to suppose that as yet he had any doubts about his own religion. We gather, indeed, from his writings that he had already passed through severe mental conflicts. Although the conviction still stood fast in his mind that the blessedness of life was attainable only in the favor of God, yet his efforts to reach this coveted position by the observance of the law had not satisfied him. On the contrary, the more he strove to keep the law the more active became the motions of sin within him; his conscience was becoming more oppressed with the sense of guilt, and the peace of a soul at rest in God was a prize which eluded his grasp.

Still he did not question the teaching of the synagogue. To him as yet this was of one piece with the history of the Old Testament, whence looked down on him the figures of the saints and prophets, which were a guarantee that the system they represented must be divine, and behind which he saw the God of Israel revealing himself in the giving of the law. The reason why he had not attained to peace and fellowship with God was, he believed, because he had not struggled enough with the evil of his nature or honored enough the precepts of the law. Was there no service by which he could make up for all deficiencies and win that grace at last in which the great of old had stood? This was the temper of mind in which he returned to Jerusalem, and learned with astonishment and indignation of the rise of a sect which believed that Jesus who had been crucified was the Messiah of the Jewish people.

CHAPTER ONE

Thank You for my Brain Explosion – Miracle Number One

The Independent Presbyterian Church on Highland Avenue burned on the 8th of April in 1992.

"But he said to me, 'My grace is sufficient for you, for my power is made perfect in weakness.' Therefore I will boast all the more gladly about my weaknesses, so that Christ's power may rest on me. That is why, for Christ's sake, I delight in weaknesses, in insults, in hardships, in persecutions, in difficulties. For when I am weak, then I am strong." 2 Corinthians 12:9,10

It was April 8, 1992, and the church was engulfed in flames as I parked the car a block away and ran to the scene with my cameras. It was a crisp spring day with the blue sky filled with clouds of gray smoke. I started taking pictures as fire trucks were coming from all directions to the Independent Presbyterian Church on Highland Avenue in Birmingham, Alabama. I made dramatic photographs that showed the enormous blaze with firefighters taking children out of the burning building. At the same time, I was hoping no one was hurt. Then it happened.

It started like any other headache, but within seconds, it felt as if my head was going to burst. I had to shut my eyes because the pressure was so severe - I was afraid they were going to pop out. I started screaming and fell on the ground next to some paramedics. They immediately started tending to me and asking me questions. All I could think of was how messy it was going to be when my head exploded. A reporter with the newspaper took my camera and asked me where my car was. At this point, I was going in and out of consciousness as the pain was becoming horrendous. The last thing I remember, as the tempest in my skull was reaching unbearable levels, was moving my arm in circles, and telling the reporter that my car was "over there." Then everything went black.

They rushed me to the hospital and performed a CAT scan, which showed a bleed the size of an apple in my lower midbrain. They hooked me up to all kinds of machines and told my wife the likelihood of my making it was slim. I had suffered a ruptured aneurysm in my brain. If I did survive, it was almost certain that I would be handicapped for the rest of my life. Knowing my life hung in the balance, my family came from New York and as far as Syria. Everyone converged on Montclair Baptist Hospital in Birmingham, where I was placed under the care of Dr. Randolph George, a neurosurgeon of many years.

I had been in this country since 1984. I came from Syria after being fed up with the social oppression and political corruption, and I sought a better life here. The depravity in Syria was prevalent. While some people could live with it, I had a hard time justifying the injustice. I married while in college at the University of Tennessee and graduated with a degree in Mechanical Engineering. Interested in photography, I became a photojournalist and never looked back. My love for photography grew, and I cherished affecting people's lives with my camera. In 1989, we moved to Birmingham, and I worked at the *Birmingham*

Post-Herald. By the time my brain exploded, I had exemplified the all-American family with two cars, a home, and a three-month-old baby. Everything was going as planned, or so I thought.

I did survive the critical first night, and the nights following. Three weeks later, I opened my eyes but did not speak or make any other motions. A week later I started making sounds and moving my head. Then I started thrashing around in my bed, only to fall on the floor; my right side was totally paralyzed and all movements took place with my left arm and leg. They finally had to tie me down. I would try to get out from under the belts that were strangling and suffocating me. I couldn't tell them why I was trying to get out, I just wanted to. I have no memory of that awful week, but my parents do. My mom still tears up when she tells me how happy they were that I woke up, and how sad it was to rush into the room to see me lying on the floor screaming. I do have a choppy memory of Mom's face crying as she lifted me up.

I had severe pain in my head but couldn't say anything. I would look at the nurse with tears in my eyes; she would look at me puzzled. I wanted to scream, "My head hurts." But nothing came out. At that moment, I was not conscious that I was someone with desperate needs. With the passing of another week more mobility came, and I started saying things, but the words came out in my native tongue - Arabic. There was a Jordanian engineer at the hospital who came and translated when my parents were out. Mom and Dad came from Damascus with my sister Mimi. My sister Rowaida and her husband, Imad, came from New York. They almost lived in the waiting room. They would translate what I thought was normal English, but was clearly Arabic. They were happy at least something was coming out of my mouth. "Will he ever speak English again?" was the question on my wife's mind.

A couple of weeks later, broken English finally came back, and I started moving around in a wheelchair. I remember bits and pieces of a birthday party. I did not know what a party was, or any of those people smiling big and giving me presents. I could barely talk. There was cake that intrigued me because my brain, which acted like the brain of a two-year-old, did not know what a cake was. I started sticking my fingers in the icing and licking them, and people were clapping and laughing. Some were crying.

I was on so much medicine, but the pain never went away. I would be told later that trauma to the brain takes years to dissipate. I knew very little. I had to learn how to brush my teeth, how to go to the bathroom, how to dress myself, what a cup was, what a pencil was. I would stare at things like I had seen them for the first time. Then the therapist would tell me what they were, and a million little brain connections would take place. I remember looking at a picture of a frog. I knew it was an animal, something that was slimy and said "ribbet." They told me it was a frog. I looked up with disbelief; the word sounded very strange. It still does.

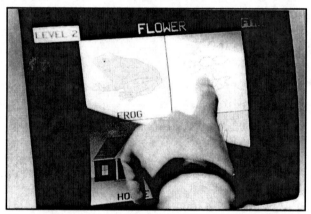

During therapy, I was asked to identify each of the pictures.

I started going to hours and hours of therapy. During one session we danced the square dance. I can laugh now as I recall how hard it was to move to music while trying not to fall. I walked to the stereo making the noise they called music. The noise made our bodies move to the rhythm, and I started touching buttons. I turned it off and everyone stopped dancing and looked at me. I turned it back on, then off again, then on. Everyone would dance while it was on, then freeze when it stopped. I was mimicking the music with my mouth. It was a bunch of adults acting like children. Later the healing of my brain would catch up with the cadence of language, and words coming out of my crooked lips started making sense.

The first time I had full memory was when two of my Syrian friends, Hisham and Asiad, were visiting from Washington, DC. We went to lunch somewhere in Birmingham, and I was very sleepy. We went back to the hospital and the next thing I remember was waking up with a severe pain in the back of my head. This pain was different; it was on the outside of my skull towards my upper neck. After asking the nurse, she said, "Oh, they put a shunt in your brain."

"Huh?" was my response, "What is a shunt?"

Dr. George explained to me later that my spine, which normally drains the fluid from my brain, was clogged up from the scar tissue. So I fell asleep for two days and they had to install a shunt, a tiny pipe that goes from the middle of my brain to my bowels.

The Road to Recovery

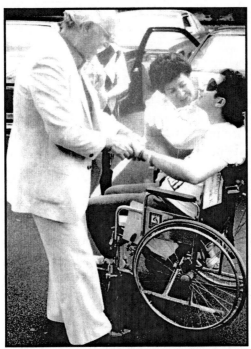

I lived in a wheel chair for a couple of months.
Here, Mom and Dad are helping me get around.

My right side was paralyzed, resulting in a crooked smile;
my double vision caused me to wear an eye patch.

My memory started working after the surgery, and every day many other faculties came back. Little by little, I started to say full sentences and feed myself. Every day, they would tell my wife to be prepared for the progress to stop, since that was the norm. I began to walk on my own. I began to smile at funny things, cry at sad things, and stare at strange things. I found much of what is considered normal to most people very bizarre, like the fact that we have to fill and empty our bodies all the time. I wondered why we were not like machines, which operate for years before needing maintenance. I would stare at my food for the longest time and wonder if I could make it without eating. Actions and sayings would go from strange to acceptable slowly. It took me longer than normal to process matters. Two versions of pain continued: one on the inside, and one on the outside. The inside pain eventually went away, but it would take two years for me to be able to touch the back of my head.

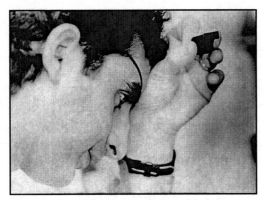

Trying to figure out what a whistle is.

I will never forget my big-hearted speech therapist, Maria. She spent hours trying to get me to recognize things as simple as a pencil, a chair, or a pair of shoes. One day, nothing was going right as I seemed to be on another planet. Frustrated, she had me hold a whistle and asked me what it was. I tried to remember the word, but I failed. I stared at the whistle, then tears came out. I was becoming aware of my deficits. She hugged me and told me it was a whistle. I looked at it, and then many connections took place, and I remembered what everything on her desk was. I looked at her and said, "You're wearing clothes." She nodded.

My progress continued at a rate higher than normal. They enrolled me in a day treatment center at Lakeshore Hospital, where the therapy ranged from occupational to physical to speech to mental. I hated it and thought I was ready to go back to work. It had been three months, and I was walking, albeit a bit languid and with a limp due to the paralysis of my right side. I remember going on little walks with my physical therapist, Nancy, along the sinuous paths around the hospital. I walked slowly while she held on to a belt around my waist. I would get tired after going about a hundred yards and would rest on a bench. One time, I looked up at a tree as an epiphany hit me and said, "treeeeee" like Forest Gump would say it. It was a very cool discovery!

Nancy laughed and repeated, "That *is* a tree Karim, very good."

I replied, "leaves." She shook her head in agreement. The walk continued.

Ebullient reporters with television stations, newspapers, and magazines did stories about me: the rare complete survival of a ruptured aneurysm victim. I would be recognized in public places, and my brain was taking me down peculiar paths. I wanted to say whatever was on my mind, such as, "What's with your hair?" or, "Why are your nails so long?" I cursed like a sailor without realizing it. Not everyone knew I had a head injury, so people looked at me funny. Some people wanted to fight with me. I did not know that telling them the truth would upset them. I was in therapy with people who had resided in their wheelchairs for over ten years. I progressed finally to leaving the hospital and returning home. By October, I went back to work and my doctor gave me permission to do whatever I wished, within reason.

I returned to my wife and my one-year-old child, who was three months old when the aneurysm took place. They told me how they would place Zade on my chest while I was in a coma, and my hand would move towards him and touch him. They also told me about the Temptations - how when they played their CD in my hospital room, my toes moved to the beat. So the doctor told them to keep the Temptations on!

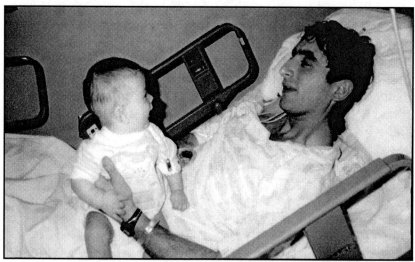

They would put Zade on my stomach when I woke up
from the coma and my arm would go up to touch him.

Moment of Illumination

*Dr. Randolph George inspired me
to search for the reason of my survival.*

During our last meeting, and after all the medical talk, Dr. George held me by my shoulders, looked into my eyes, and said with a low and serious voice, "In my years as a neurosurgeon, I have seen very few people recover as you did. You have to find out why you survived."

I looked at him passively and said, "OK, I will." But I didn't really understand the miracle that took place.

He shook my shoulders again and repeated, "You have to find out why."

This time I stared back at him and said with a solemn voice, "I will."

Those words from Dr. George haunted me for a long time.

How was I going to find out? No one else knew why I made it. What am I to do?

Note: I have talked with Dr. George recently and he remembered my case. When I reminded him of what he said to me, he replied, "Aren't we all supposed to figure out why we are here?" He has retired and is farming corn and soybeans along the Chesapeake Bay.

I had a slight idea why I made it, but I was too scared to divulge the thought, even to myself. My hospital room wall was covered with prayers from individuals and churches. I always wondered why those Christians were praying for a Muslim man. I had a feeling that God saved me to tell the story about His love. Friends would lead me to pastors who would say similar things: "God wants to show His love through you." And "God saved you for a reason, you will discover the reason in due time." When? When was I going to discover the reason? And why was I thriving against all odds?

I started photographing again at the newspaper while wearing an eye patch. Two permanent side effects became a daily thing. The first is my double vision. I had three eye muscle surgeries to correct the double vision caused by the bleed. The brain was unable to lock the eye muscles in, so I have to live seeing two of everything. I just ignore it. If I am not thinking about it, I see fine just with my right eye. I simply tell people that I see twice as good as anyone else. Another side effect was my short-term memory. If I met someone without making an effort to remember who they were, the name evaporated right after they said it. Things got better eventually. I still have to repeat the name in my head a few times. Despite those deficits, I am so blessed to be walking and talking. I take every day as a gift, and every breath as possibly my last. Life is so delicious when you live that way. Many people take this beautiful life for granted, not knowing it can all go away in a split second.

The Early Years of Islam

Men are not allowed to enter the mosque
with their shoes when they are ready to pray.

Most women pray in their homes.

I grew up a Muslim adhering to all mores of the religion. I feared Allah as I was supposed to do. I attended *Salah* (prayer at the mosque five times a day) when I could: once at dawn, once at noon, once in the afternoon, once at sunset, and once after sunset. I did the *Wudu* before every prayer (the washing of hands, face, arms, and feet required to purify oneself). Prayer consisted of standing and facing Mecca, the place where the prophet Muhammad is buried, then reciting verses and sayings while bending and kneeling. The prayer ends with sitting and looking to the right and saying, *Al-Sallam Aliekom Warahmato Allah* (Peace and Allah's mercy be with you), and then repeating those beautiful words while looking to the left.

I fasted, *Soum*, the month of Ramadan from sunrise to sunset without consuming any food or drink. In the summer, the water bottles looked too good in the refrigerator! What's a little boy to do when he is told he can't drink water all day? The month of Ramadan was one of my favorites. Mom made lots of delicious food. We would sit at the table waiting for the sunset call to prayer, *Adhan*. Upon hearing the first words: *Allah O'Akbar Allah O'Akbar* (God is great God is great), we were allowed to break the fast. And break the fast I did, devouring everything in sight!

I tried my best to understand the esoteric law and ritual in Islam, but my brain wanted to be free from it all. I was scared to share these thoughts with anyone, except my father. He was a renowned poet and a writer, and we would discuss religion for hours. He told me that Islam was the last religion, and it is the one we should stick with, but to keep studying and exploring. While I loved and respected my father, I also longed for a loving relationship with God. Why was I supposed to be afraid of Him? Does he love us?

Another ritual I did not comprehend was bloody: *the Tadhia* (the slaughter of a lamb). How does the blood of an animal grant us forgiveness? I will never forget the first time I saw this. I was about eight or nine, and our neighbors downstairs decided to slaughter a sheep on *Eid-Al-Adha* (the feast when all Muslims celebrate returning from the *Hajj* – the Pilgrimage to Mecca that Muslims are required to do once in their lifetime). Unknown to me, the sacrifice was taking place in their back yard right under our balcony.

The butcher dragged the sheep by its head and two front feet and laid it on the ground while it continued to kick and bleat. It was a shock to see the butcher put his knee on the sheep and slit its throat with a small knife. So much blood shot out of the animal, splattering everywhere and scaring me to death. I ran outside the house only to be greeted by another terrifying sight: there was a stream of dark, brownish red blood running down along the curb. I shrieked and ran back inside. My father held me while I kicked and screamed in reaction to the sickening scene outside.

On a regular basis, I attended the *Hallaqa*, a circle of boys taught by the Imam at the mosque. We would learn to recite the Quran and memorize verses as well as sayings of the prophet Muhammad. We wore the white Islamic dress, *Ghalabia*, and the little round hats, *Taeiah*. For a while I became a seriously devout Muslim who couldn't get enough. I loved walking to the mosque for the dawn prayer while most people were asleep. I would then try to stay awake as the Imam called for the *Hallaqa*. Occasionally, I would stumble across something in the Quran I did not understand. The Imam would explain it, and I would shake my head affirming, but my thirst for the truth was never quenched.

My faith journey started as those discords turned into major questions later in adulthood, and as I realized that surviving my aneurysm was more than a chance happening. But looking back at my life, God had other plans. He saved my life once before the aneurysm - before I was born.

Your Journey

"And we know that for those who love God all things work together for good, for those who are called according to his purpose."
Romans 8:28

_____

_____

_____

_____

_____

_____

_____

_____

_____

_____

_____

_____

_____

_____

_____

Saul the Persecutor
by James Stalker

State of the Christian Church.—Christianity was as yet only two or three years old, and was growing very quietly in Jerusalem. Although those who had heard it preached at Pentecost had carried the news of it to their homes in many quarters, its public representatives had not yet left the city of its birth. At first the authorities had been inclined to persecute it, and checked its teachers when they appeared in public. But they had changed their minds and, acting under the advice of Gamaliel, resolved to neglect it, believing that it would die out, if let alone. The Christians, on the other hand, gave as little offence as possible; in the externals of religion they continued to be strict Jews and zealous of the law, attending the temple worship, observing the Jewish ceremonies and respecting the ecclesiastical authorities.

It was a kind of truce, which allowed Christianity a little space for secret growth. In their upper rooms the brethren met to break bread and pray to their ascended Lord. It was the most beautiful spectacle. The new faith had alighted among them like an angel, and was shedding purity on their souls from its wings and breathing over their humble gatherings the spirit of peace. Their love to each other was unbounded; they were filled with the inspiring sense of discovery; and, as often as they met, their invisible Lord was in their midst. It was like heaven upon earth. While Jerusalem around them was going on in its ordinary course of worldliness and ecclesiastical asperity, these few humble souls were felicitating themselves with a secret which they knew to contain within it the blessedness of mankind and the future of the world.

But the truce could not last, and these scenes of peace were soon to be invaded with terror and bloodshed. Christianity could not keep such a truce; for there is in it a world-conquering force, which impels it at all risks to propagate itself, and the fermentation of the new wine of gospel liberty was sure sooner or later to burst the forms of the Jewish law.

At length a man arose in the Church in whom these aggressive tendencies embodied themselves. This was Stephen, one of the seven deacons who had been appointed to watch over the temporal affairs of the Christian society. He was a man full of the Holy Ghost and possessed of capabilities which the brevity of his career only permitted to suggest but not to develop themselves. He went from synagogue to synagogue, preaching the Messiahship of Jesus and announcing the advent of freedom from the yoke of the law. Champions of Jewish orthodoxy encountered him, but were not able to withstand his eloquence and holy zeal. Foiled in argument, they grasped at other weapons, stirring up the authorities and the populace to murderous fanaticism.

Stephen.—One of the synagogues in which these disputations took place was that of the Cilicians, the countrymen of Paul. May he have been a rabbi in this synagogue and one of Stephen's opponents in argument? At all events, when the argument of logic was exchanged for that of violence, he was in the front. When the witnesses who cast the first stones at Stephen were stripping for their work, they laid down their garments at his feet. There, on the margin of that wild scene, in the field of judicial murder, we see his figure, standing a little apart and sharply outlined against the mass of persecutors unknown to fame—the pile of many-colored robes at his feet, and his eyes bent upon the holy martyr, who is kneeling in the article of death and praying: "Lord, lay not this sin to their charge."

The Persecutor.—His zeal on this occasion brought Paul prominently under the notice of the authorities. It probably procured him a seat in the Sanhedrin, where we find him soon afterward giving his vote against the Christians. At all events, it led to him being entrusted with the work of utterly uprooting Christianity, which the authorities now resolved upon. He accepted their proposal; for he believed it to be God's work. He saw more clearly than any one else what was the drift of Christianity; and it seemed to him destined, if unchecked, to overturn all that he considered most sacred. The repeal of the law was in his eyes the obliteration of the one way of salvation, and faith in a crucified Messiah blasphemy against the divinest hope of Israel. Besides, he had a deep personal interest in the task. Hitherto he had been striving to please God, but always felt his efforts to come short; here was a chance of making up for all arrears by one splendid act of service. This was the iron of agony in his soul which gave edge and energy to his zeal. In any case he was not a man to do things by halves; and he flung himself headlong into his task.

Terrible were the scenes which ensued. He flew from synagogue to synagogue, and from house to house, dragging forth men and women, who were cast into prison and punished. Some appear to have been put to death, and—darkest trait of all—others were compelled to blaspheme the name of the Savior. The Church at Jerusalem was broken in pieces, and such of its members as escaped the rage of the persecutor were scattered over the neighboring provinces and countries.

It may seem too venturesome to call this the last stage of Paul's unconscious preparation for his apostolic career. But so indeed it was. In entering on the career of a persecutor he was going on straight in the line of the creed in which he had been brought up; and this was its reduction to absurdity. Besides, through the gracious working of Him whose highest glory it is out of evil still to bring forth good, there sprang out of these sad doings in the mind of Paul an intensity of humility, a willingness to serve even the least of the brethren of those whom he had abused, and a zeal to redeem lost time by the parsimonious use of what was left, which became permanent spurs to action in his subsequent career.

CHAPTER TWO

Thank You for Saving My Birth - Miracle Number Two

Mom and Dad spent time in Europe for their honeymoon.

"In Damascus there was a disciple named Ananias. The Lord called to him in a vision, 'Ananias!' 'Yes, Lord,' he answered. The Lord told him, 'Go to the house of Judas on Straight Street and ask for a man from Tarsus named Saul, for he is praying. In a vision he has seen a man named Ananias come and place his hands on him to restore his sight.' 'Lord,' Ananias answered, 'I have heard many reports about this man and all the harm he has done to your holy people in Jerusalem. And he has come here with authority from the chief priests to arrest all who call on your name.' But the Lord said to Ananias, 'Go! This man is my chosen instrument to proclaim my *name to the Gentiles and their kings and to the people of Israel. I will show him how much he must suffer for my name.' Then Ananias went to the house and entered it. Placing his hands on Saul, he said, 'Brother Saul, the Lord—Jesus, who appeared to you on the road as you were coming here— has sent me so that you may see again and be filled with the Holy Spirit.' Immediately, something like scales fell from Saul's eyes, and he could see again. He got up and was baptized, and after taking some food, he regained his strength." Acts 9:10-19*

Kherridean Shamsi-Basha spotted Laila Chalak walking in the Muhajereen neighborhood of Damascus in the mid 1950s. He was 40 and she was 23. Back then, men had to be financially established in order to get married and pay the dowry, Mahr. He turned around and followed the beautiful woman with striking black hair and almond-shaped eyes. After some investigative work, he learned about her family and came with his mother to ask for her hand. During the engagement, his lucid poetry, illustrious social status, and fervent eloquence turned Mom's head. They were wed a short time later and spent two months in Europe on a honeymoon, and their life continued to be a honeymoon until Dad died in 2005.

They had three children: my sister Rowaida, my brother Maher, and my other sister Mimi. Mom was finished with children and was depressed after Mimi was born. Dad had been working many hours and traveling. He had a successful clothing store and would make several buying trips to Europe every year. He loved poetry and would write on the side. Later in life he would become a renowned poet and a writer in Syria. Their life seemed to be easing off a little with the youngest reaching the one-year mark; Mom thought she was sailing into normality. Then one day she awoke throwing up. The throwing up continued. She went to the doctor, without telling Dad, to discover she was pregnant . . . with me.

Depression came back like a monster and she went crazy: "Not another child." Her life was just starting to be pleasant. They lived in a charming section of the city and had friends and acquaintances. Dad's work was going well. They would have parties where fifty to sixty people would come and stay till the wee hours of the morning. Dad had his friends, and she had hers. Dad would have Nadwe (a round table once a month.) It was the Who's Who in the Arab world from ambassadors to professors to doctors to engineers. Anyone who was anyone would come, and they would sit in a huge circle and discuss political, social, scientific, and a myriad of academic matters. They would deliberate critical discourses with ease and mastery.

I used to sneak into the guest room adorned with the best furniture in the house, and reserved for when "important" people came over, to steal some of the scrumptious food Mom had prepared. Sometimes I would get caught and laughter would erupt – while some faces remained serious. Other times I would retreat to my favorite hiding spot under the chair Dad occupied. I would listen to the chatter, understanding very little, and enjoying Dad using big words. The next morning I would wake up in my own bed wondering how I got there.

It was different when Mom had her friends over. The food was plentiful, and everything had to be perfect. And while Dad and his associates discussed serious issues, Mom and her friends talked about clothes, belly danced, and gossiped about others. I was usually ordered to go somewhere and play with my friends, which was a welcome edict any given time. Except for the tempting food situation – and the belly dancing which was fun, and a little racy to watch.

Stealing some Kibbe!

Mom lavishly prepared foods we did not see every day: From balls of *Kibbe* (lamb and wheat bulgur mixed together then fried), to *Muhamaera* (a red pepper paste), to *Yabra* (stuffed grape leaves), to cakes and petit fours and *Beruk* and *Maamool* (sweet treats) and deliciousness on a plate! My friends and I would scheme to acquire items from the sumptuous cornucopia. Plans would range from faking injuries, to peeking through the keyhole, to plain running and grabbing then escaping without getting caught.

Had Mom not had me, she would have been in the clear as far as her social life was concerned. Another child would ruin everything. She contemplated the situation with her altered foresight and decided to go to her doctor to discuss an abortion, but not before confiding in her best friend, Hanrietta. She had to unload on someone before the big event.

Abortion Bound

My son Dury during the first few seconds after his birth.

*Hanrietta (Fourth from right) during my sister's
birthday party. My father is holding me.*

Mom made Hanrietta promise to keep quiet and drive her to
the doctor's office. Then she told her to stay in the car and went
upstairs to the waiting room. Hanrietta was sitting in the car fuming: "How can I let my best friend go through with an abortion?"
Then she would convince herself that she was being a good friend.
Mom was about to go in to see the doctor when Hanrietta finally
walked through the door, pulled mom out by her hair, and threw
her into the car. Not a word was uttered as they drove back to the
house, although many tears flowed from both of them. Several
months later, I was born.

Mom told me the story while she and my sister Mimi were
visiting me the summer of 1995. She was sitting in my house in
Birmingham smoking her morning cigarette with the fancy European cigarette holder. She inhaled, let out a big puff of smoke,
and looked at me and said, "Yeah, you almost didn't make it." I
laughed and said, "I know, the aneurysm was close." She looked at
me with a half smiling/half serious face and said, "No, you were
almost not born." Then she proceeded to tell me the whole story.

I was stunned. I did not know what to think. She kept smoking
and sipping her coffee like she had just talked about a movie she
saw the day before. To me this movie was a close call with death.
I had mixed feelings about the tale: on the one hand, Mother's depression took hold of her and distorted her judgment. On the other, how can anyone abort a living baby? Part of me understands

the situation may not be right for the mother to have the baby, be it rape or other reasons. While acknowledging these ideas, I will never condone aborting a baby at any stage of pregnancy. No matter what the circumstances are. The quintessential life God ordained should be allowed to flourish. You can always put the child up for adoption. I don't know if Mom would have gone through with the abortion had it not been for Hanrietta. Who knows, this book might never have existed.

Despite the raging feelings inside of me after Mom told me the tale, a smirk came as I remembered Hanrietta, the woman who scared me to death in my youth. She was built big with broad shoulders and a huge face like a horse. Everything about her was scary to a little boy. She would immediately start looking for me when she came to visit, and would grab me before I could run away. Then she would start kissing me and squeezing me while I screamed and flailed around. She kept kissing me with those big horse lips, making slobber go everywhere. Finally she would put me down, and I would run like the wind. When I knew she was coming, I would escape or hide under my bed until she gave up.

The Trouble Maker

My mother, left, tried to ignore my mischief.

Having breakfast with the family at our condo.

After my birth, Mom overcame her depression and was very thankful to Hanrietta for preventing the abortion. We grew up in a loving house full of affection from my father and discipline from my mother. As I became a young boy about eight or nine years old, I remember always innocently misbehaving and getting in trouble with Mom, only for Dad to save the day. Whatever trouble I would come across, Mom always caught me and pulled my ear. That was her favorite punishment, and it hurt.

My oldest sister Rowaida was the model child. She always did what she was told, and her grades were perfect. She never misbehaved, and she loved me dearly and felt sorry for me when cornered by Mom. My brother Maher was another story. He defied Mom, and unlike me, who escaped conflict, he would verbally fight with Mom head-on. They would yell at each other, and he was too big for an ear pull. My sister Mimi was the spy who reported to Mom all of my infractions. Mimi and I were in a constant war.

Peace was a rare thing at our house. All four children were in one bedroom at first. Eventually we graduated to one room for the boys, another for the girls. Maher would forbid me from entering the room if he had friends over, and I would go crying to Dad. I would then walk into the room and taunt him, and he would chase me. Maher and I would revel in forbidden activities, be it food we were not supposed to eat, or places we were not supposed to go. Mom always found out and would punish us. We exhausted all the ways she could have found out. Then we discovered Mimi's CIA connection to Mom. She told her everything while tricking us into doing the deed. Rowaida stayed out of it all, and was a peacemaker. She still is.

I will never forget one day I came home with a bad grade on a test. Mimi saw the test and smiled arrogantly saying, "Wait till Dad sees this, you are in trouble *Ya Habeeby.*"

She always followed her remarks with *Ya Habeeby* (my loved one), as Dad made it well known the title was mine.

I looked at the test and said, "I won't get in trouble if I sign it myself instead of Dad, you won't tell on me, will you?"

She was confused for a minute, then intending the opposite she said, "I won't tell, I promise."

I scribbled Dad's signature right in front of her. Then my ADD took over. I left the test right there on the table and ran to play with the kids outside. Next thing I knew, all my friends stopped playing and stared behind me with fear in their eyes. I froze, thinking this could not be good. I felt Mom's hand grab my ear and pull me straight to Dad. She had the test in her other hand, and Mimi was standing right next to Dad, smiling. Dad looked at the test, then he asked Mom and Mimi to leave. He imparted his wisdom about always doing the right thing, the line he told me every time I did wrong. Then he hugged me and sent me off.

My Sanctuary

My father's stomach was where I felt the safest.

On a regular and daily basis, I would misbehave, and Mom would chase me screaming: *Taa ya Efreet* (Come here you little ghost). I would run into the library, where Dad would be sitting on his favorite chair reading. Never slowing down, I would continue my run towards him, and without hesitation he would open his *abaya* (camel hair house robe) widely. I would dive into his chest as he covered me completely and returned to reading. Seconds later, Mom would enter the room and ask my whereabouts, and Dad would deny seeing me. The library had two doors, and he would say that I might have slipped out the other door.

Listening to his heartbeat from my dark and cozy cocoon, I would hear Mom moving chairs around looking for me. Filled with doubt and wonderment about my constant vanishing, she would abandon the library and go look somewhere else. Dad would start laughing, and his chest vibrated with a welcoming noise. He would unfold the abaya saying, "We did it again." Then he would squeeze me so tightly I could hardly breath. This continued for a year or two, until I got big enough for Dad's stomach to look rather large. One day, Mom stared at it with narrowed eyes, felt me from over the abaye and said, "Aha, this is where the little Efreet has been hiding." My sanctuary with Dad was discovered, but he would remain my refuge into adulthood.

Hanrietta treated me like Dad did, with amazing grace. She would stand in between Mom and me pleading, "He won't do it again, I know it. I promise this is the last time he will ever do *that*."

"That" could have been one of about 100 things I did that Mom didn't like. Like walking into the house with my shoes on - we were supposed to take them off at the door. Or hiding the dirty clothes under piles of clean clothes, or messing with Mimi to get her in trouble, or pulling Mimi's hair, or touching Mimi, or looking at Mimi, or breathing around Mimi. Mimi was Mom's favorite, and I was Dad's and Hanrietta's.

Painting the Fence

Me at age ten, always in trouble!

Hanrietta gave me the book *Tom Sawyer*, and told me that I resembled Tom. I devoured the book and read it many times. I wanted to be like that boy with his constant mischief. One day, I would get caught doing a *Tom*-deed, and Mom gave me the verdict: "Karim, tomorrow you will pull the weeds out of the garden as punishment for your actions." My head was spinning. Pull weeds? On Friday? (The weekend in the Arab world). Fridays were devoted to escaping the house early and playing soccer and riding bikes until the dinner hour. Then getting pulled by the ear into the house and dumped in the bathtub. That night, I went to bed reading Tom Sawyer for the tenth time.

The next day and just like she had announced, Mom showed me the bountiful weeds. I started pulling for an hour or so, and my friends who had heard of the injustice started trickling in. First up was Suhail, a pudgy fellow who loved to play goalie for the sole reason of not having to run. He looked at me with squinted eyes to make sure he wasn't dreaming and said, "Oh my God, it is true. Are you going to do this all day?"

"Yaah" I said, "I get to pull weeds today instead of boring play time."

Suhail's face showed a confused look: "Are you serious?"

he said, "You mean to tell me you'd rather pull weeds than play . . . com'on."

I continued pulling weeds while whistling, "Yeah . . . No play today, got to do this very important task. Not everyone can do this you know."

Suhail looked at me with doubtful eyes, "I can pull weeds if I wanted to" he said.

"Not really Suhail," I said, "you got to know which is weed and which is not. It is not just pulling; it takes a ton of strength."

"I am plenty strong, let me show you," he said with enthusiasm.

I looked at the brand new soccer ball and said, "How about trading that ball for an hour?"

He contemplated then said, "OK, but don't lose it. My brother would kill me."

He jumped into the garden and started working. Next came brothers Faddy and Faisal. A similar conversation took place. I got a coke and a candy bar, and they were doing my dirty work. After a couple of hours, I was down the street playing, eating, drinking, and laughing when I heard Mom scream. I looked towards the house to see Mom watching six boys pulling weeds with no Karim in sight.

Hanrietta knew the rebel in me, and she not only saved my life, she made me realize that every action we take can have huge consequences. We should strive to "Do the right thing" always, and have the courage to take a stand against "The wrong thing" ...Always

Hanrietta did, and I will forever be grateful.

Your Journey

"And whatever you do, in word or deed, do everything in the name of the Lord Jesus, giving thanks to God the Father through him." Colossians 3:17

The Dramatic Conversion of Paul
by J. Gresham Machen

Paul was an apt pupil of Gamaliel. He advanced in the Jews' religion beyond any of his own age among his countrymen, 'being more exceedingly zealous for the traditions' of his fathers (Galatians 1:14). His zeal displayed itself especially in the persecution of the Christian Church (Philippians 3:6). Various reasons may be suggested for Paul's opposition to the Church.

In the first place, Jesus was not the kind of Messiah that Paul was looking for. Paul expected a Messiah who should be a glorious king upon the throne of David. Instead of that, the Messiah of the Christians was a miserable criminal; a poor, weak man, at least, who could not even save himself from the executioner. The form of his death was singularly shameful. If that was the only kind of Messiah there was, then the hope of Israel was dead! The belief of the Christians seemed to be horrible blasphemy against the precious promises of God.

In the second place, Paul opposed Christians because he was devoted to the law. In that he was a genuine Pharisee (Phil. 3:5). Pharisaism was essentially a law religion. Fulfill the law of God, said the Pharisees, and you will be saved. In itself, that principle was perfectly correct. But the trouble was that the Pharisees were satisfied with a very imperfect sort of fulfillment of the law. They went on the principle that the more separate commandments you fulfill, the more surely you win salvation. So they multiplied the commandments even far beyond the Old Testament. But they did not see clearly enough that all their obedience, even to the weightiest commandments, was hopelessly imperfect. They sought to earn their salvation. They did not see that in view of human sinfulness, salvation, if it comes at all, can come only by the free gift of God. Pharisaism was a law religion. Christianity— and Paul was keen enough to see it—was entirely different. Though the Christians continued to observe the Mosaic law, they were really depending for their salvation, not upon their obedience, but solely upon their faith in the crucified Savior. If the Christians were right, then the Pharisees' law-righteousness was wrong, and the Jews, with their law, were not much better off than sinners of the Gentiles; the exclusive position of Israel was destroyed.

Before Paul was converted, he was not gradually coming nearer to Christianity. If anything, he was moving farther off. It is true, we must not suppose that he was altogether satisfied with his condition. He was no hypocrite. He was earnestly striving after righteousness. And probably he was dissatisfied, in his heart of hearts, with the measure of righteousness what he had attained. But the more he became dissatisfied, the greater would become his devotion to the law and the more earnest his opposition to the Christians. If his obedience was not perfect enough, it must be made more perfect just by rooting out the blasphemous sect. The persecution of the Christians seemed to be a meritorious work, which would earn for Paul the favor of God.

In persecuting the Christians Paul thought he was doing God service. He "did it ignorantly in unbelief" (1 Tim. 1:13). That, however, was no adequate excuse. The persecution of the church was deadly sin. Paul himself came to regard it as such (1 Cor. 15:9; 1 Tim. 1:15). And Paul was perfectly right. Not only his persecution of the Church but also his whole Pharisaic life was sinful. It was better than most lives are, but still it was sin. It was an effort to buy heaven by the imperfect righteousness of man. A futile effort! The power of sin was too strong. Even if Paul wanted to do good, evil was present with him. His whole inner life was impure. His soul was really in rebellion against God. In other words, he was just like the rest of men—a guilty sinner under God's wrath and curse.

Paul's Dramatic Conversion

And yet he attained salvation. It came in the strangest way. He was at the height of his persecuting zeal. He was making havoc of the Church of God, Gal. 1:13. He had consented at the death of the first Christian martyr, Acts 7:58; 8:1; 22:20; 26:10. He was breathing threatening and slaughter, Acts 9:1. Not satisfied with the destruction that he had wrought in Jerusalem, he obtained authority from the Sanhedrin to extend the persecution to Damascus.

And then, suddenly, when it was least expected, the wonderful thing happened. Paul was nearing Damascus with his companions. It was midday. Suddenly a light more intense than the light of the sun shone around him. His companions saw the light. But Paul saw more than they. He saw the Lord Jesus Christ, 1 Cor. 9:1; 15:8; Acts 9:17,27; 22:14; 26:16. He became a witness to the resurrection. His companions heard a voice; but Paul alone understood what was said, Acts 9:7; 22:9. It was the voice of the Lord calling him to be a servant and an apostle. It was useless to resist. Jesus had broken every barrier down. "It is hard for thee to kick against the goad," Acts 26:14. The crucified Teacher whom Paul had despised was really risen from the dead, the Lord of glory, the true Messiah of Israel. The shameful death on the cross was really the divine sacrifice for the sins of men.

All Paul's life crumbled away beneath him. In miserable blindness he groped his way into Damascus, a poor, wretched, broken-spirited man! All his zeal had been nothing but rebellion against the King of Israel. Yet Jesus had appeared to him, not to put him to shame, but to save him. The poor, bewildered, broken-spirited rabbi became the most influential man in the history of the world.

The Meaning of the Conversion

Paul's conversion shows that Christianity is a supernatural thing. Up to the conversion Paul's life had been a natural development, but the conversion itself was a sudden blaze of glory. It is very much the same with all of us. True, the form of Christ's appearing is very diverse. We do not see him with the bodily eye. We do not, like Paul, become witnesses to the resurrection. Many of us do not know when we first saw him. It is a great mistake to demand of every man that he shall be able, like Paul, to give the day and hour of his conversion. Many men, it is true, still have a definite experience. It is not pathological. It may result in glorious Christian lives. But it is not universal, and it should not be induced to tactless methods. The children of Christian homes often seem to grow up into the love of Christ. When they decide to unite themselves definitely with the Church, the decision need not necessarily come with anguish of soul. It may simply be the culmination of a God-enriched childhood, a recognition of what God has already done rather than the acquisition of something new.

In any case, however, Christian experience is not just a continuation of the old life, but the entrance of something from the outside. Many men are content with this world. Like the youthful Jew of Tarsus, they are content with doing what other men do. But Christianity is contact with the unseen and eternal. Its beginning in the soul cannot be predicted and cannot be explained. Paul was a persecutor of Christ's followers. We, too, are sinners. But Christ met Paul on the way to Damascus, and he meets us, too, today. We cannot explain why he should receive us. We do not deserve it. But he does receive us, and then he gives us work to do. Paul, the Christian, was still able to use all the preparation of his years at Tarsus and all of his Jewish training in Jerusalem. But after Christ appeared to him he used them not for earth but for heaven. Christ will treat us as he treated Paul. Whatever our walk in life, be it exalted or be it humble, Christ can make it worthwhile. After the vision came the apostleship. There is big work for all of us, if only Christ be our leader. The true Christian life, no matter how humble, is never commonplace. It brings, first, the joy of peace with God, and second, the joy of work that is worthwhile.

CHAPTER THREE

Did God Make Man, or Did Man Make God?

*A nun at a third-century monastery
in the mountains northwest of Damascus.*

*"For it is by grace you have been saved, through faith—and this is not from
yourselves, it is the gift of God— not by works, so that no one can boast. For
we are God's handiwork, created in Christ Jesus to do good works, which
God prepared in advance for us to do." Ephesians 2:8-10*

Eighth grade at Al-Thaqafi Middle School in Damascus was one of
my least favorite years. It was a tough school with high academic
standards. You had to be erudite and astute to get ahead, and I was
the poster child for attention deficit disorder. My concentration
would veer off the subject at the slightest distraction. Sometimes
I made up my own distractions. There was also Mr. Hashem, my
religion teacher, who almost rendered me faithless with his harsh
criticism. I was full of questions, and he was short-tempered. He
was a tall balding man with a huge nose and skinny chin. He had

a belly, but all his other body parts were narrow and boney. My questions were in the safe zone – tolerated by Mr. Hashem that is - until I met my Christian friend Moneir.

Christians make up 15-20% of the Syrian population and live side by side with Muslims. You might find a church right next to a mosque. Of course things are changing currently with the unrest and civil war in Syria, and no one knows what will happen when the dust, and bullets, settle. Persecution of Christians is on the rise in a country torn by civil war and factions fighting for supremacy. More than 100,000 have died, and more will die until one day, hopefully soon, peace reigns - as was the case in my childhood.

The Bab Touma gate still stands in the Christian section of Damascus.

In my teenage years, freedom of religion was the norm. My friends and I would go to *Bab Touma,* where the Christians lived, and where the Street Called Straight is (the one mentioned in the book of Acts). It is also the place where the Apostle Paul was lowered over the wall in a basket. *Bab Touma* means the Gate of Thomas. We would go there for one reason: the girls were so pretty, and they did not cover their hair! Later I would meet Moneir from *Bab Touma,* who would become a close friend.

Moneir sat behind me at school and protected me from bullies. We did everything together. We built a tree house from an old refrigerator pallet, which became our escape from reality. We spent hours in the tree talking about our dreams and the girls playing next door, whom we could see through the leaves. We were both in love with Hazzar, but we never talked about it. She had dark hair the color of night and green, emerald eyes. She treated us the same, but I wanted more, and I am sure Moneir did as well. But wanting more from the same *woman* did not matter. We remained friends.

We would wrestle on the grass and make mud castles. Mom would scream in horror when I entered our condo black and brown from the dirt and with mud caked on my clothes. We would play cops and robbers, cowboys and Indians, and whatever two groups that were at war. We fashioned weapons out of sticks and ropes and rubber bands. We made guns that shot little marbles. During the summer, I either slept at his house, or he slept at mine. Dinnertime was interesting with the Christian prayer. Muslims say, *Besm Allah Arrahman Arraheem* (In the name of God the merciful the compassionate). At Moneir's house, everyone would close their eyes and hold hands, then his father would start praying. When I was there, they prayed in the name of God. Moneir told me they normally prayed in the name of Jesus, but his dad wanted me to feel included. I would peek to see the faces all austere and wonder, What are they thinking?

We would talk about everything from girls to school to traveling overseas together to escaping on our bikes, never to be seen again. Occasionally we would talk about religion. He wanted to share his faith with me, and I had a lot of questions: Why are there so many religions? How do you know the right one? Who was Jesus? Why did He have to die? If He was God, why didn't He save himself? And what about the thing you call "The Trinity"? Huh? Three things and one thing at the same time? Moneir had some answers, but they were typical for a thirteen-year-old boy: short and confused. And just like me, he was full of questions. He asked me about Islam, and why we had to do all the stuff like praying five times a day and fasting. And why we believed in a religion that sent us to hell for our sins. Is there forgiveness in Islam? Was there love in Islam? Why did we fear God? I would elaborate with long and scattered explanations, and eventually we would leave each other totally dissatisfied.

During one of those conversations, Moneir said something about "love" being the reason we are here on this earth. That God loved us so much, and He wants us to love Him back; and another thing about a *heart operation* when you become a believer. Of course I wanted no part of a heart operation, or any other operation on any of my organs. But "love" was an interesting concept. Why didn't Islam teach more about that?

The Road to Heaven

Moneir told me something that irritated Mr. Hashem when I asked, "How come Christians go to Heaven without doing anything, while we have to do all that work?" Mr. Hashem looked at me that day from behind his thick glasses, and I could see his whole face tense up,

"I am going to assume that by 'work' you mean the five pillars of Islam: prayer, fasting, the pilgrimage, giving money to the poor, and reciting the *Shahada* (The saying that makes you a Muslim, *La ilaha illa illah, Muhammad rasulul lah* (There is no god but God, Mohammad is the messenger of God.) We just have to do those things Kari'eem, (He always stretched my name, probably because he liked me so much!). Then on judgment day, the good is weighed against the bad, and if you pass, you go to Heaven."

"And what if you don't pass?" I asked.

His voice raised an octave as he yelled, "Then you go to hell. There are varying degrees of hell, and the length of time depends on how much bad you have done." He was totally irked.

Moneir had told me something else - that when you believe in Jesus, you are forgiven past, present, and future . . . forever . . . just for believing. I let Mr. Hashem calm down for a few days, then on a day when he seemed to be in decent mood, I asked,

"How come Christians are forgiven forever, while we are punished for our sins?"

He looked at me with disbelief. "More questions about Christians?" he said with an agitated voice. He then started to lose his grip on the class as some of the students were echoing my questions. He screamed:

"You are forgiven if God chooses to forgive you; you still have to work and earn your place in Heaven. No one goes to Heaven for doing nothing, and no one is forgiven forever. Now everyone shut up and open your books to chapter four, the prophet Muhammad, *Salla Allah Alaihe Wasallam* (Peace be upon him)."

I felt totally insatiable but decided to let it go, "Maybe one day I will attain the answer to these questions. Or maybe I will wonder no more. I will just become a good Muslim boy without curiosity. Curiosity was, according to Mr. Hashem, of the devil. Maybe he was right."

The Question

One day, the discussion was the early life of the prophet Muhammad, how he spent much time in a cave where the angel Gabriel conveyed the Quran to him. After getting nowhere with my questions, I started doodling in my notebook. Mr. Hashem was going on and on when I thought, "Maybe I will become a believer in a different religion. What about Buddhism or Hinduism? When are we going to learn about those? I would make a good Buddhist." Raji next door was Indian, and he told me about Buddhism, and how your soul keeps coming back to inhabit another form. The thought scared me a bit at first, but something about it was appealing until one day he said, "If you have been bad, you can come back as a three-legged cat." That was it. Buddhism was out.

I kept drawing funny faces and writing jokes, when my arm decided to detach from my body and write a question that petrified me. What was I thinking? I knew I had issues, but this question had more than "issues" - it shook my faith to its foundation. I slammed the notebook shut. What I did not realize was that shutting the notebook hard was loud enough for the teacher to stop talking, and for the entire class to turn and look.

I tried to brush it off so I would attract no attention, but my face tuned red, and Mr. Hashem stared at me. He wore the kind of glasses that hid his eyes. If you asked a question, you just assumed he was looking at you. I knew he was fixed upon me like a rattlesnake. He slowly walked over to my desk, grabbed the notebook from under my shaky hand, and walked back to his desk.

He sat down and read what I had written on the last page. A slow and a huge smile came upon his face. He has been trying hard to catch me all year.

"Kari . . . eeem." He sang my name with much pleasure. "Please come up front."

I got up and walked to the front of the class, wishing the ground would open up and swallow me. There were smirks and laughter from the students. He handed me my notebook and said, "Please read to the class what you wrote on the last page."

I took the notebook and faced the class. There was a good bit of noise, which I welcomed, so with a hushed voice I recited the question. No one heard a thing.

"I want everyone to shut up," Mr. Hashem screamed. "Read it again . . . with a loud voice."

"Did God make man, or did man make God?" I said quivering.

You could have dropped a pin and heard it. A hush fell upon the class and there were some gasps. Mr. Hashem grabbed his paddle from the drawer and gave me ten good licks. Then he took me to the principal's office, where I received ten more good licks. They gave me a note for Dad to sign, and I returned to class. It hurt to sit down, but I held the tears back. You were not supposed to cry when paddled at school, although this time they put a lot of gusto into it.

The bell finally rang and I imagined hearing Dad harping on me for writing the inconceivable question. I slowly walked home to see Dad's wool hat through the window of the library. He was writing, which could have been good or bad. He could be too busy to deal with such an offense, or he could be just in the mood. I sighed and walked in straight to his desk with my head lowered. He stopped writing and gave me a hug saying, "What is the matter *Habeeby*?"

I handed him the piece of paper and waited. He read it and said, "What is this question about God that caused a problem?"

I swallowed, then whispered,

"Did God make man, or did man make God?" I tried to read his face.

His expression ranged from shocked at first, to a little disturbed, to greatly disturbed, to just plain awestruck. I couldn't decipher where he settled. He finally said, "That is a provocative question my son. I think God is trying to communicate with you by arousing such wonderment in your soul. He does the same with me. Occasionally I wonder. Keep pursuing an answer to your gratification, but I can give you my take: It is a lot *easier to live* knowing that God made man."

He seemed to be pleased with the answer, and I was happy he did not turn the matter over to Mom, where an ear pull would have been a sure thing. I started to walk out of the library, only to stop and turn around saying, "I don't want just *easier to live* Dad," and I walked out.

I finished high school but was eager to change scenery. Syria was mired in corruption and the United States seemed to be calling my name!

YOUR JOURNEY

"Finally, brothers, whatever is true, whatever is honorable, whatever is just, whatever is pure, whatever is lovely, whatever is commendable, if there is any excellence, if there is anything worthy of praise, think about these things." Philippians 4:8

_____

_____

_____

_____

_____

_____

_____

_____

_____

_____

_____

_____

_____

_____

_____

_____

Paul Prepared to Preach the Gospel to the World
by James Stalker

Sojourn in Arabia.—When a man has been suddenly converted, as Paul was, he is generally driven by a strong impulse to make known what has happened to him. Such testimony is very impressive; for it is that of a soul which is receiving its first glimpses of the realities of the unseen world, and there is a vividness about the report it gives of them which produces an irresistible sense of reality. Whether Paul yielded at once to this impulse or not we cannot say with certainty. The language of the book of Acts, where it is said that "straightway he preached Christ in the synagogues," would lead us to suppose so. But we learn from his own writings that there was another powerful impulse influencing him at the same time; and it is uncertain which of the two he obeyed first. This other impulse was the wish to retreat into solitude and think out the meaning and issues of that which had befallen him. It cannot be wondered at that he felt this to be a necessity. He had believed his former creed intensely and staked everything on it; to see it suddenly shattered in pieces must have shaken him severely. The new truth which had been flashed upon him was so far-reaching and revolutionary that it could not be taken in at once in all its bearings. Paul was a born thinker; it was not enough for him to experience anything; he required to comprehend it and fit it into the structure of his convictions.

Immediately, therefore, after his conversion he went away, he tells us, into Arabia. He does not, indeed, say for what purpose he went; but, as there is no record of his preaching in that region and this statement occurs in the midst of a vehement defense of the originality of his gospel, we may conclude with considerable certainty that he went into retirement for the purpose of grasping in thought the details and the bearings of the revelation he had been put in possession of. In lonely contemplation he worked them out; and, when he returned to mankind, he was in possession of that view of Christianity which was peculiar to himself and formed the burden of his preaching during the subsequent years.

There is some doubt as to the precise place of his retirement, because Arabia is a word of vague and variable significance. But most probably it denotes the Arabia of the Wanderings, the principal feature of which was Mount Sinai. This was a spot hallowed by great memories and by the presence of other great men of revelation. Here Moses had seen the burning bush and communed with God on the top of the mountain. Here Elijah had roamed in his season of despair and drunk anew at the wells of inspiration. What place could be more appropriate for the meditations of this successor of these men of God? In the valleys where the manna fell and under the shadows of the peaks which had burned beneath the feet of Jehovah he pondered the problem of his life.

It is a great example. Originality in the preaching of the truth depends on the solitary intuition of it. Paul enjoyed the special inspiration of the Holy Ghost; but this did not render the concentrated activity of his own thinking unnecessary but only lent it peculiar intensity; and the clearness and certainty of his gospel were due to these months of sequestered thought. His retirement may have lasted a year or more; for between his conversion and his final departure from Damascus, to which he returned from Arabia, three years intervened; and one of them at least was spent in this way.

We have no detailed record of what the outlines of his gospel were till a period long subsequent to this; but, as these, when first they are traceable, are a mere cast of the features of his conversion, and, as his mind was working so long and powerfully on the interpretation of that event at this period, there can be no doubt that the Gospel sketched in the Epistles to the Romans and the Galatians was substantially the same as he preached from the first; and we are safe in inferring from these writings our account of his Arabian meditations.

Failure of Man's Righteousness.—The starting-point of Paul's thinking was still, as it had been from his childhood, the conviction, inherited from pious generations, that the true end and felicity of man lay in the enjoyment of the favor of God. This was to be attained through righteousness; only the righteous could God be at peace with and favor with His love. To attain righteousness must, therefore, be the chief end of man.

But man had failed to attain righteousness and had thereby come short of the favor of God, and exposed himself to the divine wrath.

Paul proves this by taking a vast survey of the history of mankind in pre-Christian times in its two great sections—the Gentile and the Jewish.

The Gentiles failed. It might, indeed, be supposed that they had not the preliminary conditions for entering on the pursuit of righteousness at all, because they did not enjoy the advantage of a special revelation. But Paul holds that even the heathen know enough of God to be aware of the obligation to follow after righteousness. There is a natural revelation of God in His works and in the human conscience sufficient to enlighten men as to this duty. But the heathen, instead of making use of this light, wantonly extinguished it. They were not willing to retain God in their knowledge and to fetter themselves with the restraints which a pure knowledge of Him imposed. They corrupted the idea of God in order to feel at ease in an immoral life. The revenge of nature came upon them in the darkening and confusion of their intellects. They fell into such insensate folly as to change the glorious and incorruptible nature of God into the images of men and beasts, birds and reptiles. This intellectual degeneracy was followed by still deeper moral degeneracy. God, when they forsook Him, let them go; and, when His restraining grace was removed, down they rushed into the depths of moral putridity. Lust and passion got the mastery of them, and their life became a mass of moral disease. In the end of the first chapter of Romans the features of their condition are sketched in colors that might be borrowed from the abode of devils, but were literally taken, as is too plainly proved by the pages even of Gentile historians, from the condition of the cultured heathen nations at that time. This, then, was the history of one half of mankind: it had utterly fallen from righteousness and exposed itself to the wrath of God, which is revealed from heaven against all unrighteousness of men.

The Jews were the other half of the world. Had they succeeded where the Gentiles had failed? They enjoyed, indeed, great advantages over the heathen; for they possessed the oracles of God, in which the divine nature was exhibited in a form which rendered it inaccessible to human perversion, and the divine law was written with equal plainness in the same form. But had they profited by these advantages? It is one thing to know the law and another thing to do it; but it is doing, not knowing, which is righteousness. Had they, then, fulfilled the will of God, which they knew?

Paul had lived in the same Jerusalem in which Jesus assailed the corruption and hypocrisy of scribes and Pharisees; he had looked closely at the lives of the representative men of his nation; and he does not hesitate to charge the Jews in mass with the very same sins as the Gentiles; nay, he says that through them the name of God was blasphemed among the Gentiles. They boasted of their knowledge and were the bearers of the torch of truth, the fierce blaze of which exposed the sins of the heathen; but their religion was a bitter criticism of the conduct of others; they forgot to examine their own conduct by the same light; and, while they were repeating, Do not steal, Do not commit adultery, and a multitude of other commandments, they were indulging in these sins themselves. What good in these circumstances did their knowledge do them? It only condemned them the more; for their sin was against light. While the heathen knew so little that their sins were comparatively innocent, the sins of the Jews were conscious and presumptuous. Their boasted superiority was therefore inferiority. They were more deeply condemned than the Gentiles they despised, and exposed to a heavier curse.

The truth is, Gentiles and Jews had both failed for the same reason. Trace these two streams of human life back to their sources and you come at last to a point where they are not two streams but one; and, before the bifurcation took place, something had happened which predetermined the failure of both. In Adam all fell, and from him all, both Gentiles and Jews, inherited a nature too weak for the arduous attainment of righteousness; human nature is carnal now, not spiritual, and, therefore, unequal to this supreme spiritual achievement.

The law could not alter this; it had no creative power to make the carnal spiritual. On the contrary, it aggravated the evil. It actually multiplied offenses; for its clear and full description of sins, which would have been an incomparable guide to a sound nature, turned into temptation for a morbid one. The very knowledge of sin tempts to its commission; the very command not to do anything is to a diseased nature a reason for doing it. This was the effect of the law: it multiplied and aggravated transgressions. And this was God's intention. Not that He was the author of sin; but, like a skillful physician, who has sometimes to use appliances to bring a sore to a head before he heals it, He allowed the heathen to go their own way and gave the Jews the law, that the sin of human nature might exhibit all its inherent qualities, before He intervened to heal it. The healing, however, was His real purpose all the time: He concluded all under sin, that He might have mercy upon all.

CHAPTER FOUR

The Road From Damascus to America

My father celebrates my graduation
from the University of Tennessee.

"But Saul increased all the more in strength, and confounded the Jews who lived in Damascus by proving that Jesus was the Christ. When many days had passed, the Jews plotted to kill him, but their plot became known to Saul. They were watching the gates day and night in order to kill him, but his disciples took him by night and let him down through an opening in the wall, lowering him in a basket." Acts 9:22-25

I started my senior year in high school with no graduation plans. I was disgusted by the corruption in government trickling down to all walks of life including school. If your dad or brother was in the army or worked at an important government position, you sailed through school without a worry in the world. Hard work could still result in advancement. But knowing the right people was more important.

That was the least of things. We had to attend military training once a week. We also had the option of attending a weeklong
summer boot camp, which reflected on our grades. All that would
have been fine had I believed in the Syrian army. During the 70s
and 80s, and even today, Syria and Israel are at odds. I hated war
and wanted peace to reign, so doing military activities was not my
favorite. I would watch people praising a suicide bomber in Israel
that killed many innocent people. Then Israel would retaliate and
kill more innocent people. Who was the winner of that back-and-
forth violence? No one. As far as I was concerned, peace was the
only way for Israelis and Palestinians to live together. The land
is plenty big, and I never understood why they couldn't agree - or
why peace is a distant dream.

The issue regarding the Promised Land dates way back. It is
true that during WWI and WWII, part of the land was given to
the Jews to live in peace with their neighbors. But they kept on
expanding and dislocating Arabs, and Arabs kept on fighting. In
my opinion, neither side did what was needed: sit around a table and talk instead of shoot at each other. Truthfully, the issue
dates back further than WWI and WWII. It dates as far back as
Abraham. Arabs contend that the child Abraham was about to
sacrifice was Ishmael, giving the Promised Land to them. Jews
and Christians believe it was Isaac, making the land rightly the
Jews'. That issue will never be resolved. So thousands of years
later, why can't we live together peacefully?

I also never understood the government in Syria and the systematic brainwashing they intended with young folks. We had to
recite sayings every morning that praised the government, *Weh-
da, Horiah, Ishterakia* (Unity, Freedom, Socialism). The government in Syria was a dictatorship hinting on socialism with a high
degree of exploitation. And while most people tried to live hon-
estly, you had to bribe and cheat to attain basic amenities like gas,
water, electricity, and food. Everyone had to show allegiance to
the president. We had our own version of freedom, "restricted
freedom." I basically felt like a ball and chain was attached to my
ankle. You couldn't accomplish what you desired. You had to do
what *they* would let you do, or what everyone in your family want-

ed you to do. Opportunities were limited. Everything hinged on whom you knew.

We had to participate in the *Maseera* (Marches), which celebrated different occasions like the independence from France or winning the 1973 war against Israel. We had to line up early and wait. Then we had to walk in step and shout things like *Berrouh, beddum, nafdeek ya Hafez,* (We sacrifice our souls and blood for you Hafez). Hafez Assad was the president, and his giant pictures were everywhere. We had to show our homage, even though deep down many hated him. People struggled to survive. We were OK since we had some money after Dad sold a house. If you didn't have money, you were out of luck. Dad had a saying: "If you have money, you could live like a king in Damascus."

The Good, The Bad, and The Ugly

*Downtown Damascus amid the hustle
and bustle of a few million people.*

Not everything about Syria was awful: The people were genuine. They would give you the shirt off their backs. Generosity was huge, and while some people had little, they would take the food that was intended for their children and feed their guests instead. You could knock on a door unannounced and spend the night, or several nights, at the house of your acquaintances without a question being asked. We constantly had people sleeping at our house. Mom was known for her delicious cooking, and she worked very hard to keep Dad's head held high in the class-divided Syrian society.

At one point in time, Arabian civilization spread over three continents from Asia to the Middle East to North Africa and even to Spain. The Islamic Golden Age was from the eighth to the twelfth centuries during the Abbasid period. Arabs led the world in discoveries of science, medicine, physics, and philosophy. Arabic literature flourished, with the Quran being considered the finest of the Arabic language. The genre continues with poets and writers to this day making their mark in worldwide venues. Many Nobel Laureates were from the Arab world, including Naguib Mahfouz for literature, and others in chemistry, physics, and political activism like former Egyptian leader Anwar Sadat and Palestinian politician Yasser Arafat.

Muslim and non-Muslim scholars translated the world's knowledge into Arabic. The Arab world was a collection of cultures that advanced knowledge gained from ancient Roman, Persian, Greek, and Byzantine civilizations. I don't know what happened to result in a declining Arab world today that is fractured at best. I am well aware of what a detriment the Ottoman Empire was to Arabs, followed by the colonization from Europe after WWI. But why haven't Arabs elucidated that democracy and rule by the people for the people is best?

Hafez Assad was a dictator whose son is currently the president. Bashar Assad "won" the elections, which were far from free and fair. Since he was educated in England, he opened the country towards the West, and people started to actually like him until the revolution, which started in 2011. Bashar Assad has slaughtered more than 100,000 people and is repeating what his father did. In 1982, there was a tiny revolution in the city of Hamah. Hafez Assad surrounded the city with tanks and killed more than 10,000 people. Those leaders are power hungry and acquire the best the country has to offer. The army extorts the leftovers, leaving the scraps to the majority of hard-working people.

Growing up in the middle of all of that was not always negative. I had great friendships that would flourish and blossom until today. Some of those friendships were from the Boy Scouts, my daily escape from reality during my teenage years.

Boy Scouts

Me (third from left) with my Boy Scout troop. The man behind me (with white hat) is Asiad Kunaish, who helped me come to the United States later.

After high school, Dad gave me the green light to leave Syria. My former Boy Scout troop leader had made his home in Knoxville, Tennessee, to obtain an MBA. So I contacted Asiad, and I would be accepted into the Engineering School at The University of Tennessee. Asiad was my favorite leader in Troop 29. We camped in the beautiful Syrian mountains during breezy summers and snowy winters. I owe the Boy Scouts a lot of what I am today. I spent eight years scouting and learned how to survive in the wilderness. I also learned how to motivate young people to do things they couldn't think possible, like hiking fifteen miles per day, or staying up all night on guard duty, or cooking for sixty people on a wood fire, or sleeping under the stars. The brotherhoods I established in the Boy Scouts would eventually get me to the United States.

I will never forget our last campout. We were not supposed to take any food, just water. And we were to spend seven nights eating off the land. We managed the first couple of days picking edible weeds and worms and fat and juicy grubs. Then we learned how to set a trap, which caught what some thought was a bunny rabbit. Except this bunny rabbit did not have big fluffy ears, it had small pointy ones. It did not have a knobby fluffy tail, it had a long wiry one. All it had in common with a bunny was its size. I was convinced that we caught a big fat rat, while others insisted it was a mountain bunny.

"Mountain bunnies look different," said one of the campers.

"Yeah, they have wiry tails like this little fellow. Look how fat he is," said another.

We cooked the beast and ate it. It was tough and very unsatisfying. I didn't mind the grubs; they were juicy, and the hunger made them taste OK despite the fact they were sticky and gross. I did learn plenty during that trip – brotherhood and endurance and tenacity and perseverance. I also learned that a week of hunger in the wilderness makes you appreciate what you have in normal life. I came back devouring everything Mom put in front of me. Memories from that camp are still with me.

I was on guard duty one cold and clear night from two to five in the morning. I kept staring at the sky wondering who made all those stars. My best friend Ziad was on guard duty with me. We laid on the ground and tried to count the infinite stars. We stopped at a hundred, then we sat there infatuated with a sight we don't see in the city. All I could think of was *how*, how can a God make all of this? And out of what? How did everything begin? We studied science in school and it provided some answers. But no one could tell me how everything got started. They just said, "God made everything."

We got up early the next day and hiked up a mountain that overlooked part of Lebanon. We spotted Syrian tanks rolling along the dirt road below, and we were scared. We stayed low until they passed. You could hear them struggle up the mountain, throwing rocks and dirt everywhere. They got close to us before heading in the other direction. I will never forget hiding and acting like we were in war with our own people. If they had seen us, they would have questioned us about being so close to the border. Syria had taken control of much of Lebanon to "protect" the country from Israel. It was not until 2005 that Syria was finally forced out of Lebanon.

During my last days in Damascus, all of my friends were taking me out for one last hurrah before Karim's big trip to America.

We talked about the disturbing situation in Syria, and how you couldn't even dream about things like independence and social and political aspirations. You were lucky to bag a pound of bread without standing in line for two hours. Long lines were the norm in a congested city of a few million people. It has the modern advances of Western civilization, but some minds were preserved in Eastern centuries past.

Parting Words

I still remember the trip to the airport. Mom was crying, and Dad was lecturing me about what *not* to do. He said, "Do anything you want, but don't marry an American. And don't forget about your country and your family and your language . . . and your religion." He would venture into how I was going to make him proud when I became an engineer, and then he would come back to, "Don't ever forget that you are a Muslim, and you will always be a Muslim. Don't let the West make you forget. I know you have always had questions, but believe me, Islam is a much better religion than Christianity. At least you have a measured way of knowing where you stand. In Christianity, it's all about a vague idea of someone dying for you two thousand years ago. It makes no sense."

I nodded. I was not too concerned with religion at the moment. I was excited at the possibilities of a country dramatized on television to have plenty of opportunities. We watched *Magnum P.I.*, *The Cosby Show*, *American Bandstand*, and other shows that gave us a cinematic picture of what America was. Unlike in Syria, *You could make any dream come true in America.* I wanted to dive into the culture. So what if I was around Christians? I knew I was a Muslim and I was proud of it. I didn't have to explain if the radical Muslims made Islam look bad and killed a bunch of innocent people every couple of years. I was of the moderate Muslim variety that condemned such actions.

I arrived in Knoxville on January 17, 1984. The temperature was fifteen degrees, and I thought I was going to freeze into a statue. The newspaper the next day would have read: "Arab

Freezes to Death Upon Arrival." Asiad picked me up and asked if I was hungry. "How about some little hamburgers?" he said. I did not know what he meant by *little* hamburger. We didn't have any hamburgers in Syria, and I was thrilled to taste a real one. We stopped by a Krystal and he ordered twelve burgers. I told him he was crazy for thinking we can eat twelve hamburgers. We finally obtained the steaming bag, and I pulled one out and about fainted from the heavenly smell. I devoured the little burger in two bites, and the next one, and the next one. I ate all twelve by myself, and Asiad was laughing the entire time. I would repeat this action the next day, and the next, until I had my fill of little Krystal burgers.

Welcome to America

I quickly acclimated to the American culture and enrolled at the Mechanical Engineering School at UT, which was not a major of my choosing. My Dad wanted me to be an engineer so he could say: "My son, the *engineer*." I pressed on to keep him happy. During my second year I met the woman that became my wife and quickly fell in what I thought was love. Being twenty years of age, I really had no idea what love was, or at least the love that goes beyond the physical. After marriage, I was quickly introduced to massive doses of Christianity. I would attend church with my wife and her family, and I enjoyed the worship experience as a family. I also liked the happiness everyone at church seemed to exude. I remained Muslim though, and was open to going to church and celebrating Christmas and Easter. I actually loved Christmas, mainly because of the gifts. Sure, it was a giving time of the year, and sure, you were supposed to think of Christ's birth and of others. But for me, the gifts were what made it special.

Another thing I was infatuated with was the honor system. The teacher would pass the test out in class, then leave the room! If they did that is Syria, many would cheat. But here, no one did. I would watch people around me struggling for answers but never taking their books out. It was hard to do the wrong thing. Why are you compelled to do the right thing when it is not forced upon you? Is that the difference between Christianity and Islam? One is by choice, the other by law?

Many of my friends at school were Christian and would ask me questions about Islam. The West has a skewed version of the religion I claimed, affected by the media and what it chooses to cover. The Islam I grew up in does not condone flying planes into buildings, or killing innocent people, or hating people from other faiths. My Islam was a benevolent version that aspired for peace. It was not what the radical Muslims preached.

I had to educate, deny, justify, and convince every time a radical Muslim committed an act of terror. My friends would also answer some of my questions about Christianity. How is it a free gift? I had the same issues I had with my childhood friend Moneir.

The Road to Damascus

For the guys on my dorm floor, finding out I was from Damascus was sometimes shocking. "You mean you are from Damascus? As in the 'Road to Damascus'?" some would ask.

"Yes . . . we have roads in Damascus," I would reply, feeling sorry for their lack of knowledge. I would add, "It is a normal city with roads and cars and many modern things." They would chuckle and say: "No no, The *Road to Damascus*, from the Bible man." I would shake my head saying, "I don't know that story. I am a Muslim."

Little by little, I learned about the *Road*. But something I never understood about Christianity was this: How can it be so simple? There has to be a catch. There has to be something we are required to do in order to earn Salvation. I did not even know where to begin with that word: Salvation. How is the death of Jesus related to what I do? Some would tell me that He was God who wants us to believe in Him so we are forgiven. I heard, but did not listen. Or maybe I listened but did not hear.

During my senior year, I was struggling with the idea of becoming an engineer. I absolutely despised everything about it. At the same time, I got a part-time job as a photographer with the student paper at UT - *The Daily Beacon*. I had never taken pictures before. I just needed any job to make some gas money. They gave five others and me cameras and said, "Shoot anything on campus, then we will decide whom to hire."

I walked into a biology class and asked the teacher if I could take pictures. She sat me on the front row. Then she took a snake out of a bag and lifted it up right in front of me. I looked up and snapped one frame. I turned in my film, and the picture looked like a sacrificial act. I was hired on the spot. I loved photography, and I would graduate as an engineer but get a job with the *Birmingham Post-Herald* as a photojournalist. My father was disappointed, but he ultimately wanted the best for me. So he allowed it.

I met many people as a newspaper photographer. Some were pastors who were intrigued with my story. This was the year before my aneurysm, and they would ask me about Islam. I would find myself asking more questions than answering theirs. I became totally fascinated with Christianity, while going occasionally to the mosque in Birmingham and doing my prayers. I fasted some of Ramadan. I could see the value of not eating to relate to the poor, to increase your compassion, and to force oneself to think about God. But there was something more rewarding when you did things for God on your own, instead of *having* to be faithful.

My dad would write me letters and always remind me that I was a Muslim who was supposed to fast and pray. "Are you praying five time a day?" he would ask on the telephone.

"Not really, Dad, it's hard to do that while going to college," I would reply. Prayer in Islam meant you have to wash and purify yourself, spread a prayer rug facing Mecca, then bend and kneel and recite verses. I thought Christians had it made. You could pray anywhere, in any shape you were in – clean or not. I liked the freedom in the social and political realms in America - I also liked the freedom inherent in the religion. The idea that you could pray any way you choose was alluring. But my fear of God always drove me back to Islam and our ways. The concept of God as a loving Father who lives in me was a foreign idea. Replacing the God I feared with a God I loved was something I desired, but was afraid to do.

Mom and Dad came and visited me a few times. Dad would always criticize the freedom Americans have. "They have too much freedom," he would say. I thought you could either have freedom or not, and I much preferred having it. He would ask to go to the mosque and I would take him. Then he would remind me of the wonderful things about Islam.

Islam does have many wonderful traits, like the surrender, modesty, and humility it preaches. The very word "Islam" means surrender in Arabic. It is a religion based on the law and on earning your place in Heaven. There is something powerful about the ritual: It places you in the zone to pray as you stand in line and lower your head. It would be equivalent to holding your hands together in Christianity. Something about the physical drives the mental and the soulful. What I did not know at the time is that the mental and soulful realms *can* become strong enough to function on their own.

Then on April 8, 1992, my journey towards the Cross would commence by my surviving the ruptured aneurysm, leaving deeper footmarks.

Your Journey

"If then you have been raised with Christ, seek the things that are above, where Christ is, seated at the right hand of God. Set your minds on things that are above, not on things that are on earth." Colossians 3:1,2

_____

_____

_____

_____

_____

_____

_____

_____

_____

_____

_____

_____

_____

_____

_____

_____

The Pauline Gospel
and the First Missionary Journey
by James Stalker

The Righteousness of God.—Man's extremity was God's opportunity; not, indeed, in the sense that, one way of salvation having failed. God devised another. The law had never, in His intention, been a way of salvation. It was only a means of illustrating the need of salvation. But the moment when this demonstration was complete was the signal for God to produce His method, which He had kept locked in His counsel through the generations of human probation. It had never been His intention to permit man to fail of his true end. Only He allowed time to prove that fallen man could never reach righteousness by his own efforts; and, when the righteousness of man had been demonstrated to be a failure, He brought forth His secret—the righteousness of God.

This was Christianity; this was the sum and issue of the mission of Christ—the conferring upon man, as a free gift, of that which is indispensable to his blessedness, but which he had failed himself to attain. It is a divine act; it is grace; and man obtains it by acknowledging that he has failed himself to attain it and by accepting it from God; it is got by faith only. It is "the righteousness of God, by the faith of Jesus Christ, unto all and upon all them that believe."

Those who thus receive it enter at once into that position of peace and favor with God in which human felicity consists and which was the goal aimed at by Paul when he was striving for righteousness by the law. "Being justified by faith, we have peace with God through our Lord Jesus Christ, by whom also we have access by faith into this grace wherein we stand, and rejoice in hope of the glory of God." It is a sunny life of joy, peace and hope which those lead who have come to know this gospel. There may be trials in it; but, when a man's life is reposing in the attainment of its true end, trials are light and all things work together for good.

This righteousness of God is for all the children of men—not for the Jews only, but for the Gentiles also. The demonstration of man's inability to attain righteousness was made, in accordance with the divine purpose, in both sections of the human race; and its completion was the signal for the exhibition of God's grace to both alike. The work of Christ was not for the children of Abraham, but for the children of Adam. "As in Adam all died, so in Christ shall all be made alive." The Gentiles did not need to undergo circumcision and to keep the law in order to obtain salvation; for the law was no part of salvation; it belonged entirely to the preliminary demonstration of man's failure; and, when it had accomplished this service, it was ready to vanish away. The only human condition of obtaining God's righteousness is faith; and this is as easy for Gentile as Jew.

This was an inference from Paul's own experience. It was not as a Jew, but as a man, that he had been dealt with in his conversion. No Gentile could have been less entitled to obtain salvation by merit than he had been. So far from the law raising him a single step toward salvation, it had removed him to a greater distance from God than any Gentile, and cast him into a deeper condemnation. How, then, could it profit the Gentiles to be placed in this position? In obtaining the righteousness in which he was now rejoicing he had done nothing which was not competent to any human being.

It was this universal love of God revealed in the gospel which inspired Paul with unbounded admiration for Christianity. His sympathies had been cabined, cribbed, confined in a narrow conception of God; the new faith uncaged his heart and let it forth into the free and sunny air. God became a new God to him. He calls his discovery the mystery which had been hidden from ages and generations, but had been revealed to him and his fellow-apostles. It seemed to him to be the secret of the ages and to be destined to usher in a new era, far better than any the world had ever seen. What kings and prophets had not known had been revealed to him. It had burst on him like the dawn of a new creation. God was now offering to every man the supreme felicity of life—that righteousness which had been the vain endeavor of the past ages.

This secret of the new epoch had not, indeed, been entirely unanticipated in the past. It had been "witnessed by the law and the prophets." The law could bear witness to it only negatively by demonstrating its necessity. But the prophets anticipated it more positively. David, for example, described "the blessedness of the man unto whom God imputed righteousness without works." Still more clearly had Abraham anticipated it. He was a justified man; and it was by faith, not by works, that He was justified—"he believed God, and it was imputed unto him for righteousness." The law had nothing to do with his justification, for it was not in existence for four centuries afterward. Nor had circumcision anything to do with it, for he was justified before this rite was instituted. In short, it was as a man, not as a Jew, that he was dealt with by God, and God might deal with any human being in the same way. It had once made the thorny road of legal righteousness sacred to Paul to think that Abraham and the prophets had trodden it before him; but now he knew that their life of religious joy and psalms of holy calm were inspired by quite different experiences, which were now diffusing the peace of heaven through his heart also. But only the first streaks of dawn had been descried by them; the perfect day had broken in his own time.

The Old Adam and the New.—Paul's discovery of this way of salvation was an actual experience; he simply knew that Christ, in the moment when He met him, had placed him in that position of peace and favor with God which he had long sighed for in vain, and, as time went on, he felt more and more that in this position he was enjoying the true blessedness of life. His mission henceforth must be to herald this discovery in its simple and concrete reality under the name of the Righteousness of God. But a mind like his could not help inquiring how it was that the possession of Christ did so much for him. In the Arabian wilderness he pondered over this question, and the gospel he subsequently preached contained a luminous answer to it.

From Adam his children derive a sad double heritage—a debt of guilt, which they cannot reduce, but are constantly increasing, and a carnal nature, which is incapable of righteousness. These are the two features of the religious condition of fallen man, and they are the double source of all his woes.

But Christ is a new Adam, a new head of humanity, and those who are connected with Him by faith become heirs of a double heritage of a precisely opposite kind. On the one hand, just as through our birth in the first Adam's line we get inevitably entangled in guilt, like a child born into a family which is drowned in debt, so through our birth in the line of the second Adam we get involved in a boundless heritage of merit, which Christ, as the Head of His family, makes the common property of its members. This extinguishes the debt of our guilt and makes us rich in Christ's righteousness. "As by one man's disobedience many were made sinners, so by the obedience of one shall many be made righteous." On the other hand, just as Adam transmitted to his posterity a carnal nature, alien to God and unfit for righteousness, so the new Adam imparts to the race of which He is the Head a spiritual nature, akin to God and delighting in righteousness.

The nature of man, according to Paul, normally consists of three sections—body, soul and spirit. In his original constitution these occupied definite relations of superiority and subordination to one another, the spirit being supreme, the body undermost, and the soul occupying the middle position. But the fall disarranged this order, and all sin consists in the usurpation by the body or the soul of the place of the spirit. In fallen man these two inferior sections of human nature, which together form what Paul calls the Flesh, or that side of human nature which looks toward the world and time, have taken possession of the throne and completely rule the life, while the spirit, the side of man which looks toward God and eternity, has been dethroned and reduced to a condition of inefficiency and death. Christ restores the lost predominance of the spirit of man by taking possession of it by his own Spirit. His Spirit dwells in the human spirit, vivifying it and sustaining it in such growing strength that it becomes more and more the sovereign part of the human constitution. The man ceases to be carnal and becomes spiritual; he is led by the Spirit of God and becomes more and more harmonious with all that is holy and divine.

The flesh does not, indeed, easily submit to the loss of supremacy. It clogs and obstructs the spirit and fights to regain possession of the throne. Paul has described this struggle in sentences of terrible vividness, in which all generations of Christians have recognized the features of their deepest experience. But the issue of the struggle is not doubtful. Sin shall not again have dominion over those in whom Christ's Spirit dwells, or dislodge them from their standing in the favor of God. "Neither death nor life, nor angels, nor principalities nor powers, nor things present nor things to come, nor height nor depth, nor any other creature shall be able to separate us from the love of God which is in Christ Jesus our Lord."

The Pauline Gospel.—Such are the bare outlines of the gospel which Paul brought back with him from the Arabian solitudes and afterward preached with unwearied enthusiasm. It could not but be mixed up in his mind and in his writings with the peculiarities of his own experience as a Jew, and these make it difficult for us to grasp his system in some of its details. The belief in which he was brought up, that no man could be saved without becoming a Jew, and the notions about the law from which he had to cut himself free, lie very distant from our modern sympathies; yet his theology could not shape itself in his mind except in contrast to these misconceptions. This became subsequently still more inevitable when his own old errors met him as the watchwords of a party within the Christian Church itself, against which he had to wage a long and relentless war. Though this conflict forced his views into the clearest expression, it encumbered them with references to feelings and beliefs which are now dead to the interest of mankind. But, in spite of these drawbacks, the Gospel of Paul remains a possession of incalculable value to the human race. Its searching investigation of the failure and the wants of human nature, its wonderful unfolding of the wisdom of God in the education of the pre-Christian world, and its exhibition of the depth and universality of the divine love are among the profoundest elements of revelation.

But it is in its conception of Christ that Paul's gospel wears its imperishable crown. The Evangelists sketched in a hundred traits of simple and affecting beauty the fashion of the earthly life of the man Christ Jesus, and in these the model of human conduct will always have to be sought; but to Paul was reserved the task of making known, in its heights and depths, the work which the Son of God accomplished as the Savior of the race. He scarcely ever refers to the incidents of Christ's earthly life, although here and there he betrays that he knew them well. To him Christ was ever the glorious Being, shining with the splendor of heaven, who appeared to him on the way to Damascus, and the Savior who caught him up into the heavenly peace and joy of a new life. When the Church of Christ thinks of her Head as the deliverer of the soul from sin and death, as a spiritualizing presence ever with her and at work in every believer, and as the Lord over all things who will come again without sin unto salvation, it is in forms of thought given her by the Holy Ghost through the instrumentality of this apostle.

THE FIRST MISSIONARY JOURNEY

Paul's Companions.—From the beginning it had been the wont of the preachers of Christianity not to go alone on their expeditions, but two by two. Paul improved on this practice by going generally with two companions, one of them being a younger man, who perhaps took charge of the traveling arrangements. On his first journey his comrades were Barnabas and John Mark, the nephew of Barnabas.

We have already seen that Barnabas may be called the discoverer of Paul; and, when they set out on this journey together, he was probably in a position to act as Paul's patron; for he enjoyed much consideration in the Christian community. Converted apparently on the day of Pentecost, he had played a leading part in the subsequent events. He was a man of high social position, a landed proprietor in the island of Cyprus; and he sacrificed all to the new movement into which he had been drawn. In the outburst of enthusiasm which led the first Christians to share their property with one another, he sold his estate and laid the money at the apostles' feet. He was constantly employed thereafter in the work of preaching, and he had so remarkable a gift of eloquence that he was called the Son of Exhortation. An incident which occurred at a later stage of this journey gives us a glimpse of the appearance of the two men. When the inhabitants of Lystra mistook them for gods, they called Barnabas Jupiter and Paul Mercury. Now, in ancient art Jupiter was always represented as a tall, majestic and benignant figure, while Mercury was the small, swift messenger of the father of gods and men. Probably it appeared, therefore, that the large, gracious, paternal Barnabas was the head and director of the expedition, while Paul, little and eager, was the subordinate. The direction in which they set out, too, was the one which Barnabas might naturally have been expected to choose. They went first to Cyprus, the island where his property had been and many of his friends still were. It lay eighty miles to the southwest of Seleucia, the seaport of Antioch, and they might reach it on the very day they left their headquarters.

Cyprus—Change of Name.—But, although Barnabas appeared to be the leader, the good man probably knew already that the humble words of the Baptist might be used by himself with reference to his companion, "He must increase, but I must decrease." At all events, as soon as their work began in earnest, this was shown to be the relation between them. After going through the length of the island, from east to west, evangelizing, they arrived at Paphos, its chief town, and there the problems they had come out to face met them in the most concentrated form.

Paphos was the seat of the worship of Venus, the goddess of love, who was said to have been born of the foam of the sea at this very spot; and her worship was carried on with the wildest licentiousness. It was a picture in miniature of Greece sunk in moral decay. Paphos was also the seat of the Roman government, and in the pro-consular chair sat a man, Sergius Paulus, whose noble character but utter lack of certain faith formed a companion picture of the inability of Rome at that epoch to meet the deepest necessities of her best sons. In the proconsular court, playing upon the inquirer's credulity, a Jewish sorcerer and quack, named Elymas, was flourishing, whose arts were a picture of the lowest depths to which the Jewish character could sink. The whole scene was a kind of miniature of the world the evils of which the missionaries had set forth to cure.

In the presence of these exigencies Paul unfolded for the first time the mighty powers which lay in him. An access of the Spirit seizing him and enabling him to overcome all obstacles, he covered the Jewish magician with disgrace, converted the Roman governor, and founded in the town a Christian church in opposition to the Greek shrine. From that hour Barnabas sank into the second place and Paul took his natural position as the head of the mission. We no longer read, as heretofore, of "Barnabas and Saul," but always of "Paul and Barnabas." The subordinate had become the leader; and, as if to mark that he had become a new man and taken a new place, he was no longer called by the Jewish name of Saul, which up to this point he had borne, but by the name of Paul, which has ever since been his designation among Christians.

The Mainland of Asia.—The next move was as obviously the choice of the new leader as the first one had been due to Barnabas. They struck across the sea to Perga, a town near the middle of the southern coast of Asia Minor, then right up, a hundred miles, into the mainland, and thence eastward to a point almost straight north of Tarsus. This route carried them in a kind of half circuit through the districts of Pamphylia, Pisidia and Lycaonia, which border, to the west and north, on Cilicia, Paul's native province; so that, if it be the case that he had evangelized Cilicia already, he was now merely extending his labors to the nearest surrounding regions.

At Perga, the starting-point of this second half of the journey, a misfortune befell the expedition: John Mark deserted his companions and sailed for home. It may be that the new position assumed by Paul had given him offense, though his generous uncle felt no such grudge at that which was the ordinance of nature and of God. But it is more likely that the cause of his withdrawal was dismay at the dangers upon which they were about to enter. These were such as might well strike terror even into resolute hearts. Behind Perga rose the snow-clad peaks of the Taurus Mountains, which had to be penetrated through narrow passes, where crazy bridges spanned the rushing torrents, and the castles of robbers, who watched for passing travelers to pounce upon, were hidden in positions so inaccessible that even the Roman army had not been able to exterminate them. When these preliminary dangers were surmounted, the prospect beyond was anything but inviting: the country to the north of the Taurus was a vast tableland, more elevated than the summits of the highest mountains in this country, and scattered over with solitary lakes, irregular mountain masses and tracts of desert, where the population was rude and spoke an almost endless variety of dialects. These things terrified Mark, and he drew back. But his companions took their lives in their hand and went forward. To them it was enough that there were multitudes of perishing souls there, needing the salvation of which they were the heralds; and Paul knew that there were scattered handfuls of his own people in these remote regions of the heathen.

Can we conceive what their procedure was like in the towns they visited? It is difficult, indeed, to picture it to ourselves. As we try to see them with the mind's eye entering any place, we naturally think of them as the most important personages in it; to us their entry is as august as if they had been carried on a car of victory. Very different, however, was the reality. They entered a town as quietly and as unnoticed as any two strangers who may walk into one of our towns any morning. Their first care was to get a lodging; and then they had to seek for employment, for they worked at their trade wherever they went. Nothing could be more commonplace. Who could dream that this travel-stained man, going from one tentmaker's door to another, seeking for work, was carrying the future of the world beneath his robe!

When the Sabbath came round, they would cease from toil, like the other Jews in the place, and repair to the synagogue. They joined in the psalms and prayers with the other worshipers and listened to the reading of the Scriptures. After this the presiding elder might ask if any one present had a word of exhortation to deliver. This was Paul's opportunity. He would rise and, with outstretched hand, begin to speak. At once the audience recognized the accents of the cultivated rabbi: and the strange voice won their attention. Taking up the passages which had been read, he would soon be moving forward on the stream of Jewish history, till he led up to the astounding announcement that the Messiah hoped for by their fathers and promised by their prophets had come; and he had been sent among them as His apostle. Then would follow the story of Jesus; it was true, He had been rejected by the authorities of Jerusalem and crucified, but this could be shown to have taken place in accordance with prophecy; and His resurrection from the dead was an infallible proof that He had been sent of God: now He was exalted a Prince and a Saviour to give repentance unto Israel and the remission of sins.

We can easily imagine the sensation produced by such a sermon from such a preacher and the buzz of conversation which would arise among the congregation after the dismissal of the synagogue. During the week it would become the talk of the town: and Paul was willing to converse at his work or in the leisure of the evening with any who might desire further information. Next Sabbath the synagogue would be crowded, not with Jews only, but Gentiles also, who were curious to see the strangers; and Paul now unfolded the secret that salvation by Jesus Christ was as free to Gentiles as to Jews. This was generally the signal for the Jews to contradict and blaspheme; and, turning his back on them, Paul addressed himself to the Gentiles. But meantime the fanaticism of the Jews was roused, who either stirred up the mob or secured the interest of the authorities against the strangers; and in a storm of popular tumult or by the breath of authority the messengers of the gospel were swept out of the town. This was what happened at Antioch in Pisidia, their first halting-place in the interior of Asia Minor; and it was repeated in a hundred instances in Paul's subsequent life.

Sometimes they did not get off so easily. At Lystra, for example, they found themselves in a population of rude heathens, who were at first so charmed with Paul's winning words and impressed with the appearance of the preachers that they took them for gods and were on the point of offering sacrifice to them. This filled the missionaries with horror, and they rejected the intentions of the crowd with unceremonious haste. A sudden revolution in the popular sentiment ensued, and Paul was stoned and cast out of the city apparently dead.

Such were the scenes of excitement and peril through which they had to pass in this remote region. But their enthusiasm never flagged; they never thought of turning back, but, when they were driven out of one city, moved forward to another. And, total as their discomfitures sometimes appeared, they quitted no city without leaving behind them a little band of converts—perhaps a few Jews, a few more proselytes, and a number of Gentiles. The gospel found those for whom it was intended—penitents burdened with sin, souls dissatisfied with the world and their ancestral religion, hearts yearning for divine sympathy and love; "as many as were ordained to eternal life believed;" and these formed in every city the nucleus of a Christian church. Even at Lystra, where the defeat seemed so utter, a little group of faithful hearts gathered round the mangled body of the apostle outside the city gates; Eunice and Lois were there with tender womanly ministrations; and young Timothy, as he looked down on the pale and bleeding face, felt his heart forever knit to the hero who had courage to suffer to the death for his faith.

In the intense love of such hearts Paul received compensation for suffering and injustice. If, as some suppose, the people of this region formed part of the Galatian churches, we see from his Epistle to them the kind of love they gave him. They received him, he says, as an angel of

God, nay, as Jesus Christ Himself; they were ready to have plucked out their eyes and given them to him. They were people of rude kindness and headlong impulses; their native religion was one of excitement and demonstrativeness, and they carried these characteristics into the new faith they had adopted. They were filled with joy and the Holy Ghost, and the revival spread on every hand with great rapidity, till the word, sounding out from the little Christian communities, was heard all along the slopes of Taurus and down the glens of the Cestrus and Halys.

Paul's warm heart could not but enjoy such an outburst of affection. He responded to it by giving in return his own deep love. The towns mentioned in their itinerary are the Pisidian Antioch, Iconium, Lystra, and Derbe; but, when at the last of them he had finished his course and the way lay open to him to descend by the Cilician Gates to Tarsus and thence get back to Antioch, he preferred to return by the way he had come. In spite of the most imminent danger he revisited all these places to see his dear converts again and cheer them in face of persecution; and he ordained elders in every city to watch over the churches in his absence.

The Return to Antioch.—At length the missionaries descended again from these uplands to the southern coast and sailed back to Antioch, from which they had set out. Worn with toil and suffering, but flushed with the joy of success, they appeared among those who had sent them forth and had doubtless been following them with their prayers; and, like discoverers returned from the finding of a new country, they related the miracles of grace they had witnessed in the strange world of the heathen.

CHAPTER FIVE

Four Years of Total Silence

The House of Saint Ananias (also called Chapel of Saint Ananias). It is the ancient house where Saint Paul was baptized, and is located near Bab Sharqi (Eastern Gate) - at the very end of the Street Called Straight.

My aneurysm took place in the spring of 1992. By summer of 1996, I had been on an uphill journey towards the Cross. All of my essence was pointing towards His love for me, the love that saved my life. At the same time, I sought a solution to one verse in the Bible that kept me away, *"I am the way, the truth, and the life. No one comes to the Father except through me" (John 14:6).* Does that mean that if I came to the Father through Jesus, my Muslim family will be left behind? What if they don't accept Jesus? And chances are they wouldn't. What will happen then? Where will they go?

To say that I struggled with that verse would be an understatement. I tried to find someone who would paint a picture with a dash of gray in it, instead of the black and white that was all over the Bible. The issue is very clear according to the Word: If you want to go to Heaven, you have to believe in Jesus. I couldn't accept anything that granted my family a dark destiny. I spoke to many pastors who failed to clarify my enigma.

I took things lightly after the aneurism. I did not have the mental capacity to be aware of the huge dilemma facing me. A couple of years later and as I healed, my awareness of the issue became huge. I wanted to convert, but only on my terms. I wanted to thank Him for saving my life. I wanted to talk about His love for the entire world. I reveled in love as the quintessence of Christianity, instead of fear – the epitome of Islam. But how could I come to the Father alone without my family? One of the pastors I spoke with, Tim Simmons, who is more than a dear friend and a brother to me, told me that one day my family could see Christ and the light of God in me. I am all for possibilities, but what if they don't? What then?

Three years after my survival, I couldn't sleep. I became a zombie functioning and doing my photography work but detached and unsettled. I lived in an ethereal realm that kept fact and fiction intermingled with no boundaries. I knew I had to do something. I decided to read more of the Gospels, hoping they might suggest ways people from other faiths could be saved. So I read Matthew, Mark, Luke, and John; the only thing I found was more assurance that Jesus is the *only* way. I read them again, and again. Then I read the entire New Testament, only to find different ways of saying the same thing:

John 20:31: *"But these are written so that you may believe that Jesus is the Christ, the Son of God, and that by believing you may have life in his name."*

Acts 4:12: *"Salvation is found in no one else, for there is no other name under heaven given to mankind by which we must be saved."* This was a bit much – "no other name."

I Timothy 2:3, 4: *"This is good, and pleases God our Savior, who wants all people to be saved and to come to a knowledge of the truth."* This one gave me a little hope. He wants all people to be saved.

1 John 2:22, 23: *"Who is the liar? It is whoever denies that Jesus is the Christ. Such a person is the antichrist—denying the Father and the Son. No one who denies the Son has the Father; whoever acknowledges the Son has the Father also." I had to stop reading after this one. So whoever wants to acknowledge God, has to acknowledge Christ. Which is another way for saying: If you don't believe in Christ, you don't believe in God.*

Then I came across this verse in Acts, where the Apostle Paul is speaking to his jailer:

Acts 16:30, 31: *"He then brought them out and asked, 'Sirs, what must I do to be saved?'They replied, 'Believe in the Lord Jesus, and you will be saved—you and your household.'"*

The black was getting blacker, and the white was getting whiter.

Finding Some Gray

Rev. Gil Smith baptized me in the summer of 1996 at Middlebrook Pike United Methodist Church in Knoxville, Tennessee.

I took a few days off. I wanted to reflect and see why I was only finding the same assertion. I had heard that there are many contradictions in the Bible. Where are they? I decided to read the New Testament one more time. This time I sought not the obvious. I was seeking something not written with ink on paper, but with love on the tablet of my heart. I found some verses that gave me a little comfort as I interpreted them in my own vernacular:

John 10:16: *"And I have other sheep that are not of this fold. I must bring them also, and they will listen to my voice. So there will be one flock, one shepherd."* That verse meant to me that Jesus will bring people from other faiths around to believe in Him.

John 5:28, 29: *"Do not be amazed at this, for a time is coming when all who are in their graves will hear his voice and come out—those who have done what is good will rise to live, and those who have done what is evil will rise to be condemned."* Here people will be judged based on their deeds and not religion. The ones who have done well will be OK.

I knew Dad did well, and so did Mom. Of course there are a few things they have messed up in their life. Who hasn't? So what will be the result of those "bad" actions? Aren't we all bad somehow? We all mess up. Oh gosh, this verse does not really work. Who are the people who have done well? Anyone?

A friend of mine told me to read Philippians. I was astounded with the joy abundant in this short letter, and to think that the Apostle Paul wrote it from prison. I did come across a verse that gave me some comfort:

Philippians 2:10, 11: *"That at the name of Jesus every knee should bow, in heaven and on earth and under the earth, and every tongue acknowledge that Jesus Christ is Lord, to the glory of God the Father."* He said right there that every knee shall bow. That means we are all OK. Or are we?

My Near-Conversion

"In this connection I journeyed to Damascus with the authority and commission of the chief priests. At midday, O king, I saw on the way a light from heaven, brighter than the sun, that shone around me and those who

journeyed with me. And when we had all fallen to the ground, I heard a voice saying to me in the Hebrew language, 'Saul, Saul, why are you persecuting me? It is hard for you to kick against the goads.' And I said, 'Who are you, Lord?' And the Lord said, 'I am Jesus whom you are persecuting. But rise and stand upon your feet, for I have appeared to you for this purpose, to appoint you as a servant and witness to the things in which you have seen me and to those in which I will appear to you.'" Acts 26:12-16

On a warm summer day in 1996, a friend of mine suggested I meet with a pastor that might put an end to my struggle, the Reverend Frank Barker. I had doubts about anyone shedding light on a subject I had beat to death. I will go into detail about meeting Rev. Barker later, but it is worth mentioning here that his words would haunt me for more than a decade: "Your family is in the hands of God . . . What are you going to do?" I walked out and left Frank sitting there with my embarrassed friend. I didn't need any narrow-minded people telling me more revelations about faith. I will do what will make sense to *me*.

A couple of weeks later, on July 4, 1996, my wife's family was having a church picnic in their home in Knoxville. Their pastor was present. I liked Gil Smith. He spoke of Christ softly and was always upbeat and positive. He led Middlebrook Pike United Methodist Church and had known about my struggles. He came to me during the cookout and offered assistance. I was taking a huge bite of my hot dog. I looked at him with a full mouth, froze for a minute, then we both exploded in laughter. I swallowed, then I said, "I do have some questions."

We walked into the office, away from the noisy crowd, and I shared with Gil my strife with that verse. Gil spoke of making leaps, then worrying about questions, not the other way around. He said that verse would become clear after I start my journey towards Jesus. I looked at Gil, thinking it can't be this easy.

"You mean to tell me that all of my search for an answer was for nothing?" I said.

"Not for nothing. God will answer those questions as you grow in your faith. You just have to trust Him. You don't have to have an answer now," Gil said.

"So I can become a Christian without believing in that verse?" I asked with my eyes focused on Gil's soft face.

"Questions before the leap can keep you up at night. Questions after the leap will fade away," he said.

I liked what that statement implied. "Will you baptize me?" I asked.

"Karim, I would be delighted to baptize you," Gil said.

"Let me get my calendar to set a date," I said and rushed to the back bedroom.

The hallway was long and dim, and the voices from the backyard were coming through the glass doors. I was walking and thinking about the huge step I was about to take: "Am I really doing this?" Abruptly I stopped in my tracks. I felt hollow inside. All I could think of was, "Something I don't like is happening to me." I touched my stomach, making sure there was still flesh in my insides. Sweat was pouring out of my entire body. With great difficulty, I continued my walk, feeling I was inside of a pool of thick mud. I made it to the bedroom, grabbed my calendar, and slowly walked back to the office.

Gil looked at me with wide eyes and said, "Are you OK?"

Soaking wet, I collapsed in a chair and told him what happened. He smiled and said, "You have been visited by the Holy Spirit my friend."

"If this is the Holy Spirit, I don't want it to ever visit again," I replied.

We set a date and I was baptized in July of 1996 with my version of Christianity—a version that worked for me, a version that loved everyone, and where everyone of any faith was going to be saved. I took John 14:6 out of my Bible. I also took out the concept of a Savior out of my Christianity: "If He can't save my family, I don't need Him to save me."

This near-conversion officially started my journey. For the first time, I professed to be a Christian. I made the leap. And now I was waiting for the answers to my burning questions. Gil was right about the intensity of the questions fading, only to be replaced by a yearning for the truth. I dived into the Word and loved the New Testament, especially Paul's letters full of grace and faith and hope and love.

Love became an essential part of my faith-life, the love that was missing from Islam. Just to think that God sent Jesus to this earth because He loved us is beyond astounding. There were many other complicated terms that I would come to understand later, like *redemption* and *Salvation* and *sanctification* and *justification*. But *love* I reveled in and completely surrendered to feeling with my whole heart. Was this the "heart operation" Moneir talked about in my youth?

Then I started to read the Old Testament, and found another concern of huge ramifications. I kept coming across the term "The Chosen People."

I Have to Love *Them?*

"I am speaking the truth in Christ—I am not lying; my conscience bears me witness in the Holy Spirit—that I have great sorrow and unceasing anguish in my heart. For I could wish that I myself were accursed and cut off from Christ for the sake of my brothers, my kinsmen according to the flesh. They are Israelites, and to them belong the adoption, the glory, the covenants, the giving of the law, the worship, and the promises. To them belong the patriarchs, and from their race, according to the flesh, is the Christ, who is God over all, blessed forever. Amen." Romans 9:1-5

Growing up as a Muslim in Syria colored my view of Israel as a nation that took our land and dislocated our people. I would see the horror of the occupation on television, and I would hear Dad and his friends talk about the Jews as conniving people. Hating the Jews was the norm. These were the 70s and 80s, when relationships between Israel and its neighbors—Syria, Lebanon, Egypt, and Jordan—were fiery at best.

Did anyone say "Chosen People"? Out of all the people on this entire planet, the Jews were chosen by God and given that land, the land that belonged to us? How am I going to change the way I feel about them? How was I to go from near hate, to total love. I had learned about the Jewish Diaspora after the Babylonians took over the land. That exodus would repeat with millions of Palestinians after the Israeli occupation. And I thought I needed help with the "Savior" concept!

Despite the enormity of this issue, and despite the fact that forgiveness was not even a flicker on my horizon, I would set this

issue aside just as I did with the *Salvation* and *Savior* colloquial.
I became competent in covering exasperating matters with a mat
of comfort. My mat was thick and vast. The *Jews* went under the
mat with the *Savior* and *Salvation*. I remained a Christian who
went to church and raised his children to be Christian. Sure I had
questions, but who didn't? Besides, a friend told me that there is
no specific reason God chose the Jews. He had to choose someone to come to earth through. The big question is, *Why the Jews?*
I guess if he had picked the Arabs, then someone might say, *Why
the Arabs?*

While I was reading the Old Testament, God finally answered
my question that got me in trouble in eighth grade: "Did God make
man, or did man make God?" I was reading in Exodus 32 about
calf worship shortly after my near-conversion in 1996:

*"And he received it at their hand, and fashioned it with a graving tool,
and made it a molten calf; and they said: 'This is thy god, O Israel, which
brought thee up out of the land of Egypt'" (Exodus 32:4).* I stopped reading and thought of an answer I can finally live with: *"God made
man, but man has made a lot of gods."*

Now I could wrestle with the biggest issue of all: Do I tell
my family?

Keeping the Secret

A couple of years after my near-conversion, people would ask
me, "How is your family taking the news?"

My answer was, "I have not told them - I don't want to
hurt them."

I had completely transformed the most intrinsic thing in my
life without telling the people I loved the most. How could I tell
them? The conversation might go something like this:

"Hey Mom and Dad . . . Ahhhh, How are you? And how is everyone? Yeah work is going fine. Kids are great, Zade and Dury
are growing. Yesterday Dury had his first popsicle. Oh, and I have
become Christian." I could imagine volcanoes erupting and titan-
ic plates shifting in their world.

Mom would scream and tell me I was crazy. Dad would be so hurt and so ashamed of his son, his pride and joy, the apple of his eyes. "You are the one who is going to make me the proudest," he would constantly say to me.

"Sure Dad, how about this for making you proud?"

I couldn't do it. I couldn't fathom the idea of telling my family that I had completely turned my back on their beliefs. Not only that, but I had accepted a belief that denied theirs altogether. Even more, a belief that took the people we hate the most, and asked us to love them.

That was too much of a task. No one had to know about my inner struggles. I could handle them one problem at a time. Had I told my family, my father might have disowned me. Pride is taught to children as a virtue in the Arab world. It is even in our poetry. What would happen to my father's pride? It would be annihilated. He wouldn't be able to meet his friends with his head held high saying, "I have a son in America." He would have to skirt the issue and hide it. And he would deny it if the news seeped out.

And what about their relationship with me? Would they accept me as a Christian? Or would they totally forget they have a son named Karim? I couldn't imagine them denying me, but I have heard of families disowning their children because of converting from Islam to Christianity. Some converts face more than the disowning of their family. Some face imprisonments, beatings, and even death.

This is something that I will never understand, killing someone because they changed their religion. What makes anyone think they can take a life just because someone has decided to follow a different path? Some tell me that my life will be in danger after this book is published. It is hard for me to believe that any rational person who reads this book and realizes the number of times the word "love" is mentioned, would be tempted to do anything other than pray for God's love to abound.

As a mater of fact, I am going to make an appeal to all Muslims all over the world - *Allow people to be free from hard laws that degrades humanity.* The very freedom Muslims and Arabs were seeking after the Arab Spring erupted should lead to a free way of thinking. A democratic dialogue that can only improve life and make true freedom an attainable quality.

Shaming my family and the danger implicit in making my near-conversion public would keep me a closet Christian till 2008. I was content and lived a double life. Again, the mat was huge and covered all of my predicaments. I was happy and God continued speaking despite his speech falling on deaf ears.

God Speaks

*The car of Dale Earnhardt (top left) flips with others
at the Talladega Superspeedway in 1997.*

Up to my near-conversion, I have been reading both the Quran and the Bible for godly inspiration. I read about Abraham in the Quran, and how God in the last second stopped him from killing his son:

"Abraham prayed: My Lord, grant me a doer of good deeds. So We gave him the good news of a forbearing son. But when he became of age to work with him, he said: O my son, I have seen in a dream that I should sacrifice you; so consider what is your view. He said: O my father, do as you are commanded; if Allah please you will find me patient. So when they had both submitted and he had thrown him down upon his forehead, and We called out to him saying, O Abraham, you have indeed fulfilled the vision.

Thus do We reward the doers of good. Surely this is a manifest trial. And We ransomed him with a great sacrifice." (37:100–107)

I also read the same story in the Bible:

"When they came to the place of which God had told him, Abraham built the altar there and laid the wood in order and bound Isaac his son and laid him on the altar, on top of the wood. Then Abraham reached out his hand and took the knife to slaughter his son. But the angel of the Lord called to him from heaven and said, 'Abraham, Abraham!' And he said, 'Here I am.' He said, 'Do not lay your hand on the boy or do anything to him, for now I know that you fear God, seeing you have not withheld your son, your only son, from me.' And Abraham lifted up his eyes and looked, and behold, behind him was a ram, caught in a thicket by his horns. And Abraham went and took the ram and offered it up as a burnt offering instead of his son. So Abraham called the name of that place, 'The Lord will provide'; as it is said to this day, 'On the mount of the Lord it shall be provided.'" Genesis 22:9-14

Why won't God talk to me like He did with Abraham? It wouldn't be until a few years after my aneurysm that I would *see* God talking to me.

It happened in 1997 at the Talladega Superspeedway, where I was covering a NASCAR race for *Sports Illustrated* magazine. I took my place near the pits and started photographing the cars flying at 200 miles per hour. The sky was peppered with puffy clouds. I remember looking at the track at one point and noticing the shadow of the clouds move along the track. Now, that may seem normal to most people. If the clouds are moving, their shadow will move along the ground. But to me at that instant, I felt God. It was as if God was trying to tell me something. I perked up and paid attention to the cars approaching from the far right at Turn 4 – and saw a few of them turn sideways.

By the time they were in front of me, there were three or four cars flipping over each other with smoke and fire bellowing. I lifted the camera to my eyes and snapped a frame. It happened so fast I barely remember it. We had film cameras back then, so I had no idea what I shot. I shipped my film to the magazine in New York hoping the picture was in focus. By the time I received the issue on Thursday, I had given up since there were no calls from the editors. I opened it like I always do to the first three pages, where they published the best pictures of the week in sports. I stood there speechless. A picture of the wreck I witnessed with my name under it gracefully occupied two pages.

I totally forgot about the clouds till I saw them moving along the road while I was driving the next day. I stopped the car and lowered my head and reveled in the moment. "Could this be a way for God to converse with me? Did He choose the light because I am a photographer?"

The scriptures teach that God is continually communicating with us through the things that He has made, *"The heavens declare the glory of God, and the sky above proclaims his handiwork. Day to day pours out speech, and night to night reveals knowledge." Psalm 19:1,2.* Sadly, seldom do we take time to listen. God is always talking to those who love Him. He desires us to know He is always there, answering our prayers in His own time, and giving us His ultimate gift: His everlasting love—the love that cost Him His Son's life.

Life continued till the day when two giant planes hit the World Trade Center, turning this world upside down and ripping my bleeding heart out of my chest.

Flames, Smoke, and Disbelief

I was having breakfast at our house in Birmingham when a neighbor knocked on the door and told me to turn the television on. I did as the second plane disappeared into the World Trade Center. I sat down and let my cereal bowl fall on the rug. At that instant, there were two major thoughts in my brain: "Please save as many people as possible out of those buildings." I know some had to have died with that huge explosion, but please God, allow the people in the towers to get out. The second thought was one I have uttered a few times before, "Don't let them be Arabs."

As the day went on, both prayers were denied. Nearly three thousand would die. And the perpetrators were Arabs. I was sick to my stomach for days. I hid myself from being seen in public. I received looks and snide comments from strangers, and even some people that have known me for years said hurtful things. I didn't mind. Look at what happened. What those terrorists did was beyond any comprehension and human decency. It was barbaric and atrocious and would change this world forever.

On a personal level, it created a dilemma: When I came to America, I dived into this culture and soaked up all that it had to offer from realities to opportunities to dreams. And I still do. But I remained an Arab-American. I was proud of my heritage and would talk boldly about what Arabs have accomplished. Little by little, I would find myself leaning more toward American ideology. When I went home to Syria to visit in 2004, a couple of years after 9/11, I was treated like an American-Arab. My Syrian friends would criticize America and I would defend it. I discovered that I was different, not only in appearance and thoughts but also in principles and virtues.

My self-identity was vague: Arab-American or American-Arab? As big as this issue was, I had even a bigger one looming:

I had to reconcile Jesus into my life.

Your Journey

"For I consider that the sufferings of this present time are not worth comparing with the glory that is to be revealed to us." Romans 8:18

_____

_____

_____

_____

_____

_____

_____

_____

_____

_____

_____

_____

_____

_____

_____

_____

_____

_____

The Second and Third Missionary Journeys
by James Stalker

The Second Missionary Journey. In his first journey Paul may be said to have been only trying his wings; for his course, adventurous though it was, only swept in a limited circle round his native province. In his second journey he performed a far more distant and perilous flight. Indeed, this journey was not only the greatest he achieved but perhaps the most momentous recorded in the annals of the human race. In its issues it far outrivaled the expedition of Alexander the Great, when he carried the arms and civilization of Greece into the heart of Asia, or that of Caesar, when he landed on the shores of Britain, or even the voyage of Columbus, when he discovered a new world. Yet, when he set out on it, he had no idea of the magnitude which it was to assume or even the direction which it was to take. After enjoying a short rest at the close of the first journey, he said to his fellow-missionary, "Let us go again and visit our brethren in every city where we have preached the word of the Lord and see how they do." It was the parental longing to see his spiritual children which was drawing him; but God had far more extensive designs, which opened up before him as he went forward.

Separation from Barnabas.—Unfortunately the beginning of this journey was marred by a dispute between the two friends who meant to perform it together. The occasion of their difference was the offer of John Mark to accompany them. No doubt when this young man saw Paul and Barnabas returning safe and sound from the undertaking which he had deserted, he recognized what a mistake he had made; and he now wished to retrieve his error by rejoining them. Barnabas naturally wished to take his nephew, but Paul absolutely refused. The one missionary, a man of easy kindliness, urged the duty of forgiveness and the effect which a rebuff might have on a beginner; while the other, full of zeal for God, represented the danger of making so sacred a work in any way dependent on one who could not be relied upon, for "confidence in an unfaithful man in time of trouble is like a broken tooth or a foot out of joint."

We cannot now tell which of them was in the right or if both were partly wrong. Both of them, at all events, suffered for it: Paul had to part in anger from the man to whom he probably owed more than to any other human being; and Barnabas was separated from the grandest spirit of the age.

They never met again. This was not due, however, to an unchristian continuation of the quarrel; for the heat of passion soon cooled down and the old love returned. Paul mentions Barnabas with honor in his writings, and in the very last of his Epistles he sends for Mark to come to him at Rome, expressly adding that he is profitable to him for ministry—the very thing he had disbelieved about him before. In the meantime, however, their difference separated them. They agreed to divide between them the region they had evangelized together. Barnabas and Mark went away to Cyprus; and Paul undertook to visit the churches on the mainland. As companion he took with him Silas, or Silvanus, in the place of Barnabas; and he had not proceeded far on his new journey when he met with one to take the place of Mark. This was Timothy, a convert he had made at Lystra in his first journey; he was youthful and gentle; and he continued a faithful companion and a constant comfort to the apostle to the end of his life.

Unrecorded Work.—In pursuance of the purpose with which he had set out, Paul began this journey by revisiting the churches in the founding of which he had taken part. Beginning at Antioch and proceeding in a northwesterly direction, he did this work in Syria, Cilicia and other parts, till he reached the center of Asia Minor, where the primary object of his journey was completed. But, when a man is on the right road, all sorts of opportunities open up before him. When he had passed through the provinces which he had visited before, new desires to penetrate still farther began to fire his mind, and Providence opened up the way.

He still went forward in the same direction through Phrygia and Galatia. Bithynia, a large province lying along the shore of the Black Sea, and Asia, a densely populated province in the west of Asia Minor, seemed to invite him and he wished to enter them. But the Spirit who guided his footsteps indicated, by some means unknown to us, that these provinces were shut to him in the meantime; and, pushing onward in the direction in which his divine Guide permitted him to go, he found himself at Troas, a town on the northwest coast of Asia Minor.

Thus he had traveled from Antioch in the south-east to Troas in the northwest of Asia Minor, a distance as far as from Land's End to John O' Groat's, evangelizing all the way. It must have taken months, perhaps even years. Yet of this long, laborious period we possess no details whatever, except such features of his intercourse with the Galatians as may be gathered from the Epistle to that church. The truth is that, thrilling as are the notices of Paul's career given in the Acts, this record is a very meager and imperfect one, and his life was far fuller of adventure, of labors and sufferings for Christ, than even Luke's narrative would lead us to suppose. The plan of the Acts is to tell only what was most novel and characteristic in each journey, while it passes over, for instance, all his repeated visits to the same scenes. There are thus great blanks in the history, which were in reality as full of interest as the portions of his life which are fully described.

Of this there is a startling proof in an Epistle which he wrote within the period covered by the Acts of the Apostles. His argument calling upon him to enumerate some of his outstanding adventures, "Are they ministers of Christ?" he asks, "I am more; in labors more abundant, in stripes above measure, in prisons more frequent, in deaths oft. Of the Jews five times received I forty stripes save one. Thrice was I beaten with rods. Once was I stoned. Thrice I suffered shipwreck. A night and a day have I been in the deep. In journeyings often, in perils of water, in perils of robbers, in perils by mine own countrymen, in perils by the heathen, in perils in the city, in perils in the wilderness, in perils in the sea, in perils among false brethren; in weariness and painfulness, in watchings often, in hunger and thirst, in fastings often, in cold and nakedness."

Now, of the items of this extraordinary catalogue the book of Acts mentions very few: of the five Jewish scourgings it notices not one, of the three Roman beatings only one; the one stoning it records, but not one of the three shipwrecks, for the shipwreck so fully detailed in the Acts happened later. It was no part of the design of Luke to exaggerate the figure of the hero he was painting; his brief and modest narrative comes far short even of the reality; and, as we pass over the few simple words into which he condenses the story of months or years, our imagination requires to be busy, filling up the outline with toils and pains at least equal to those the memory of which he has preserved.

Crossing to Europe.—It would appear that Paul reached Troas under the direction of the guiding Spirit without being aware whither his steps were next to be turned. But could he doubt what the divine intention was when, gazing across the silver streak of the Hellespont, he beheld the shores of Europe on the other side? He was now within the charmed circle where for ages civilization had had her home; and he could not be entirely ignorant of those stories of war and enterprise and those legends of love and valor which have made it forever bright and dear to the heart of mankind.

At only four miles' distance lay the Plain of Troy, where Europe and Asia encountered each other in the struggle celebrated in Homer's immortal song. Not far off Xerxes, sitting on a marble throne, reviewed the three millions of Asiatics with which he meant to bring Europe to his feet. On the other side of that narrow strait lay Greece and Rome, the centers from which issued the learning, the commerce and the armies which governed the world. Could his heart, so ambitious for the glory of Christ, fail to be fired with the desire to cast himself upon these strongholds, or could he doubt that the Spirit was leading him forward to this enterprise? He knew that Greece, with all her wisdom, lacked that knowledge which makes wise unto salvation, and that the Romans, though they were the conquerors of this world, did not know the way of winning an inheritance in the world that is to come; but in his breast he carried the secret which they both required.

It may have been such thoughts, dimly moving in his mind, that projected themselves into the vision which he saw at Troas; or was it the vision which first awakened the idea of crossing to Europe? As he lay asleep, with the murmur of the Aegean in his ears, he saw a man standing on the opposite coast, on which he had been looking before he went to rest, beckoning and crying, "Come over into Macedonia and help us." That figure represented Europe, and its cry for help Europe's need of Christ. Paul recognized in it a divine summons; and the very next sunset which bathed the Hellespont in its golden light shone upon his figure seated on the deck of a ship the prow of which was moving toward the shore of Macedonia.

In this passage of Paul, from Asia to Europe, a great providential decision was taking effect, of which, as children of the West, we cannot think without the profoundest thankfulness. Christianity arose in Asia and among an Oriental people; and it might have been expected to spread first among those races to which the Jews were most akin. Instead of coming west, it might have gone eastward. It might have penetrated into Arabia and taken possession of those regions where the faith of the False Prophet now holds sway. It might have visited the wandering tribes of Central Asia and, piercing its way down through the passes of the Himalayas, reared its temples on the banks of the Ganges, the Indus and the Godavery. It might have traveled farther east to deliver the swarming millions of China from the cold secularism of Confucius. Had it done so, missionaries from India and Japan might have been coming to England and America at the present day to tell the story of the Cross. But Providence conferred on Europe a blessed priority, and the fate of our continent was decided when Paul crossed the Aegean.

Macedonia.—As Greece lay nearer than Rome to the shore of Asia, its conquest for Christ was the great achievement of his second missionary journey. Like the rest of the world it was at that time under the sway of Rome, and the Romans had divided it into two provinces—Macedonia in the north and Achaia in the south. Macedonia was, therefore, the first scene of Paul's Greek mission. It was traversed from east to west by a great Roman road, along which the missionary moved, and the places where we have accounts of his labors are Philippi, Thessalonica and Beroea.

The Greek character in this northern province was much less corrupted than in the more polished society to the south. In the Macedonian population there still lingered something of the vigor and courage which four centuries before had made its soldiers the conquerors of the world. The churches which Paul founded here gave him more comfort than any he established elsewhere. There are none of his Epistles more cheerful and cordial than those to the Thessalonians and the Philippians; and, as he wrote the latter late in life, the perseverance of the Macedonians in adhering to the gospel must have been as remarkable as the welcome they gave it at the first. At Berea he even met with a generous and open-minded synagogue of Jews—the rarest occurrence in his experience.

Women and the Gospel.—A prominent feature of the work in Macedonia was the part taken in it by women. Amid the general decay of religions throughout the world at this period, many women everywhere sought satisfaction for their religious instincts in the pure faith of the synagogue. In Macedonia, perhaps on account of its sound morality, these female proselytes were more numerous than elsewhere; and they pressed in large numbers into the Christian Church. This was a good omen; it was a prophecy of the happy change in the lot of women which Christianity was to produce in the nations of the West. If man owes much to Christ, woman owes still more. He has delivered her from the degradation of being man's slave and plaything and raised her to be his friend and his equal before Heaven; while, on the other hand, a new glory has been added to Christ's religion by the fineness and dignity with which it is invested when embodied in the female character.

These things were vividly illustrated in the earliest footsteps of Christianity on our continent. The first convert in Europe was a woman, at the first Christian service held on European soil the heart of Lydia being opened to receive the truth; and the change which passed upon her prefigured what woman in Europe was to become under the influence of Christianity. In the same town of Philippi there was seen, too, at the same time an equally representative image of the condition of woman in Europe before the gospel reached it, in a poor girl, possessed of a spirit of divination and held in slavery by men who were making gain out of her misfortune, whom Paul restored to sanity. Her misery and degradation were a symbol of the disfiguration, as Lydia's sweet and benevolent Christian character was of the transfiguration of womanhood.

Liberality of the Churches.—Another feature which prominently marked the Macedonian churches was a spirit of liberality. They insisted on supplying the bodily wants of the missionaries; and, even after Paul had left them, they sent gifts to meet his necessities in other towns. Long afterward, when he was a prisoner at Rome, they deputed Epaphroditus, one of their teachers, to carry thither similar gifts to him and to act as his attendant. Paul accepted the generosity of these loyal hearts, though in other places he would work his fingers to the bone and forego his natural rest rather than accept similar favors. Nor was their willingness to give due to superior wealth. On the contrary, they gave out of deep poverty. They were poor to begin with, and they were made poorer by the persecutions which they had to endure. These were very severe after Paul left, and they lasted long. Of course they had broken first of all on Paul himself. Though he was so successful in Macedonia, he was swept out of every town at last like the off-scourings of all things. It was generally by the Jews that this was brought about. They either fanaticized the mob against him, or accused him before the Roman authorities of introducing a new religion or disturbing the peace or proclaiming a king who would be a rival to Caesar. They would neither go into the kingdom of heaven themselves nor suffer others to enter.

But God protected His servant. At Philippi He delivered him from prison by a physical miracle and by a miracle of grace still more marvelous wrought upon his cruel jailer; and in other towns He saved him by more natural means. In spite of bitter opposition, churches were founded in city after city, and from these the glad tidings sounded out over the whole province of Macedonia.

Achaia.—When, leaving Macedonia, Paul proceeded south into Achaia, he entered the real Greece—the paradise of genius and renown. The memorials of the country's greatness rose around him on his journey. As he quitted Berea, he could see behind him the snowy peaks of Mount Olympus, where the deities of Greece had been supposed to dwell. Soon he was sailing past Thermopylae, where the immortal Three Hundred stood against the barbarian myriads; and, as his voyage neared its close, he saw before him the island of Salamis, where again the existence of Greece was saved from extinction by the valor of her sons.

Athens.—His destination was Athens, the capital of the country. As he entered the city, he could not be insensible to the great memories which clung to its streets and monuments. Here the human mind had blazed forth with a splendor it has never exhibited elsewhere. In the golden age of its history Athens possessed more men of the very highest genius than have ever lived in any other city. To this day their names invest it with glory. Yet even in Paul's day the living Athens was a thing of the past. Four hundred years had elapsed since its golden age, and in the course of these centuries it had experienced a sad decline. Philosophy had degenerated into sophistry, art into dilettanteism, oratory into rhetoric, poetry into verse-making. It was a city living on its past. Yet it still had a great name and was full of culture and learning of a kind. It swarmed with so-called philosophers of different schools, and with teachers and professors of every variety of knowledge; and thousands of strangers of the wealthy class, collected from all parts of the world, lived there for study or the gratification of their intellectual tastes. It still represented to an intelligent visitor one of the great factors in the life of the world.

With the amazing versatility which enabled him to be all things to all men, Paul adapted himself to this population also. In the market-place, the lounge of the learned, he entered into conversation with students and philosophers, as Socrates had been wont to do on the same spot five centuries before. But he found even less appetite for the truth than the wisest of the Greeks had met with. Instead of the love of truth an insatiable intellectual curiosity possessed the inhabitants. This made them willing enough to tolerate the advances of any one bringing before them a new doctrine; and, as long as Paul was merely developing the speculative part of his message, they listened to him with pleasure. Their interest seemed to deepen, and at last a multitude of them conveyed him to Mars' Hill, in the very center of the splendors of their city, and requested a full statement of his faith. He complied with their wishes and in the magnificent speech he there made them, gratified their peculiar tastes to the full, as in sentences of the noblest eloquence he unfolded the great truths of the unity of God and the unity of man, which lie at the foundation of Christianity. But, when he advanced from these preliminaries to touch the consciences of his audience and address them about their own salvation, they departed in a body and left him talking.

He quitted Athens and never returned to it. Nowhere else had he so completely failed. He had been accustomed to endure the most violent persecution and to rally from it with a light heart. But there is something worse than persecution to a fiery faith like his, and he had to encounter it here: his message roused neither interest nor opposition. The Athenians never thought of persecuting him; they simply did not care what the babbler said; and this cold disdain cut him more deeply than the stones of the mob or the lictors' rods. Never perhaps was he so much depressed. When he left Athens, he moved on to Corinth, the other great city of Achaia; and he tells us himself that he arrived there in weakness and in fear and in much trembling.

Corinth.—There was in Corinth enough of the spirit of Athens to prevent these feelings from being easily assuaged. Corinth was to Athens very much what Glasgow is to Edinburgh. The one was the commercial, the other the intellectual capital of the country. Even the situations of the two places in Greece resembled in some respects those of these two cities in Scotland. But the Corinthians also were full of disputatious curiosity and intellectual hauteur. Paul dreaded the same kind of reception as he had met with in Athens. Could it be that these were people for whom the gospel had no message? This was the staggering question which was making him tremble. There seemed to be nothing in them on which the gospel could take hold: they appeared to feel no wants which it could satisfy.

There were other elements of discouragement in Corinth. It was the Paris of ancient times—a city rich and luxurious, wholly abandoned to sensuality. Vice displayed itself without shame in forms which struck deadly despair into Paul's pure Jewish mind. Could men be rescued from the grasp of such monstrous vices? Besides, the opposition of the Jews rose here to unusual virulence. He was compelled at length to depart from the synagogue altogether, and did so with expressions of strong feeling. Was the soldier of Christ going to be driven off the field and forced to confess that the gospel was not suited for cultured Greece? It looked like it.

But the tide turned. At the critical moment Paul was visited with one of those visions which were wont to be vouchsafed to him at the most trying and decisive crises of his history. The Lord appeared to him in the night, saying, "Be not afraid, but speak, and hold not thy peace; for I am with thee, and no man shall set on thee to hurt thee; for I have much people in this city." The apostle took courage again, and the causes of discouragement began to clear away. The opposition of the Jews was broken, when they hurried him with mob violence before the Roman governor, Gallio, but were dismissed from the tribunal with ignominy and disdain. The very president of the synagogue became a Christian, and conversions multiplied among the native Corinthians. Paul enjoyed the solace of living under the roof of two leal-hearted friends of his own race and his own occupation, Aquila and Priscilla. He remained a year and a half in the city and founded one of the most interesting of his churches, thus planting the standard of the cross in Achaia also and proving that the gospel was the power of God unto salvation even in the headquarters of the world's wisdom.

THE THIRD MISSIONARY JOURNEY

It must have been a thrilling story Paul had to tell at Jerusalem and Antioch when he returned from his second journey; but he had no disposition to rest on his laurels, and it was hot long before he set out on his third journey.

In Asia.—It might have been expected that, having in his second journey planted the gospel in Greece, he would in his third have made Home his principal aim. But, if the map be referred to, it will be observed that, in the midst, between the regions of Asia Minor which he evangelized during his first journey and the provinces of Greece in which he planted churches in his second journey, there was a hiatus—the populous province of Asia, in the west of Asia Minor. It was on this region that he descended in his third journey. Staying for no less than three years in Ephesus, its capital, he effectively filled up the gap and connected together the conquests of his former campaigns. This journey included, indeed, at its beginning, a visitation of all the churches formerly founded in Asia Minor and, at its close, a flying visit to the churches of Greece; but, true to his plan of dwelling only on what was new in each journey, the author of the Acts has supplied us only with the details relating to Ephesus.

Ephesus.—This city was at that time the Liverpool of the Mediterranean. It possessed a splendid harbor, in which was concentrated the traffic of the sea which was then the highway of the nations; and, as Liverpool has behind her the great towns of Lancashire, so had Ephesus behind and around her such cities as those mentioned along with her in the epistles to the churches in the book of Revelation—Smyrna, Pergamos, Thyatira, Sardis, Philadelphia, and Laodicea. It was a city of vast wealth, and it was given over to every kind of pleasure, the fame of its theater and race-course being world-wide.

But Ephesus was still more famous as a sacred city. It was a seat of the worship of the goddess Diana, whose temple was one of the most celebrated shrines of the ancient world. This temple was enormously rich and harbored great numbers of priests. At certain seasons of the year it was a resort for flocks of pilgrims from the surrounding regions; and the inhabitants of the town flourished by ministering in various ways to this superstition. The goldsmiths drove a trade in little silver models of the image of the goddess which the temple contained and which was said to have fallen from heaven. Copies of the mystic characters engraven on this ancient relic were sold as charms. The city swarmed with wizards, fortune-tellers, interpreters of dreams and other gentry of the like kind, who traded on the mariners, merchants and pilgrims who frequented the port.

Paul's work had therefore to assume the form of a polemic against superstition. He wrought such astonishing miracles in the name of Jesus that some of the Jewish palterers with the invisible world attempted to cast out devils by invoking the same name; but the attempt issued in their signal discomfiture. Other professors of magical arts were converted to the Christian faith and burnt their books. The vendors of superstitious objects saw their trade slipping through their fingers. To such an extent did this go at one of the festivals of the goddess that the silversmiths, whose traffic in little images had been specially smitten, organized a riot against Paul, which took place in the theater and was so successful that he was forced to quit the city.

But he did not go before Christianity was firmly established in Ephesus, and the beacon of the gospel was twinkling brightly on the Asian coast, in response to that which was shining from the shores of Greece on the other side of the Aegean. We have a monument of his success in the churches lying all around Ephesus which St. John addressed a few years afterward in the Apocalypse; for they were probably the indirect fruit of Paul's labors. But we have a far more astonishing monument of it in the Epistle to the Ephesians. This is perhaps the profoundest book in existence; yet its author evidently expected the Ephesians to understand it. If the orations of Demosthenes, with their closely packed arguments between the articulations of which even a knife cannot be thrust, be a monument of the intellectual greatness of the Greece which listened to them with pleasure; if the plays of Shakespeare, with their deep views of life and their obscure and complex language, be a testimony to the strength of mind of the Elizabethan Age, which could enjoy such solid fare in a place of entertainment; then the Epistle to the Ephesians, which sounds the lowest depths of Christian doctrine and scales the loftiest heights of Christian experience, is a testimony to the proficiency which Paul's converts had attained under his preaching in the capital of Asia.

Principal Literary Period of the Apostle Paul.—It has been mentioned that the third missionary journey closed with a flying visit to the churches of Greece. This visit lasted several months; but in the Acts it is passed over in two or three verses. Probably it was little marked with those exciting incidents which naturally tempt the biographer into detail. Yet we know from other sources that it was nearly the most important part of Paul's life; for during this half-year he wrote the greatest of all his Epistles, that to the Romans, and two others only less important—that to the Galatians and the Second to the Corinthians.

We have thus alighted on the portion of his life most signalized by literary work. Overpowering as is the impression of the remarkableness of this man produced by following him, as we have been doing, as he hurries from province to province, from continent to continent, over land and sea, in pursuit of the object to which he was devoted, this impression is immensely deepened when we remember that he was at the same time the greatest thinker of his age, if not of any age, and, in the midst of his outward labors, was producing writings which have ever since been among the mightiest intellectual forces of the world, and are still growing in their influence.

In this respect he rises sheer above all other evangelists and missionaries. Some of them may have approached him in certain respects—Xavier or Livingstone in the world-conquering instinct, St. Bernard or Whitefield in earnestness and activity. But few of these men added a single new idea to the world's stock of beliefs, whereas Paul, while at least equaling them in their own special line, gave to mankind a new world of thought. If his Epistles could perish, the loss to literature would be the greatest possible with only one exception—that of the Gospels which record the life, the sayings and the death of our Lord. They have quickened the mind of the Church as no other writings have done, and scattered in the soil of the world hundreds of seeds the fruits of which are now the general possession of mankind. Out of them have been brought the watchwords of progress in every reformation which the Church has experienced. When Luther awoke Europe from the slumber of centuries, it was a word of Paul which he uttered with his mighty voice: and when, one hundred years ago, our own country was revived from almost universal spiritual death, she was called by the voices of men who had rediscovered the truth for themselves in the pages of Paul.

Form of his Writings.—Yet in penning his Epistles Paul may himself have had little idea of the part they were to play in the future. They were drawn out of him simply by the exigencies of his work. In the truest sense of the word they were letters, written to meet particular occasions, not formal writings, carefully designed and executed with a view to fame or to futurity. Letters of the right kind are, before everything else, products of the heart; and it was the eager heart of Paul, yearning for the weal of his spiritual children or alarmed by the dangers to which they were exposed, that produced all his writings. They were part of his day's work. Just as he flew over sea and land to revisit his converts, or sent Timothy or Titus to carry them his counsels and bring news of how they fared, so, when these means were not available, he would send a letter with the same design.

His Style.—This may seem to detract from the value of these writings. We may be inclined to wish that, instead of having the course of his thinking determined by the exigencies of so many special occasions and his attention distracted by so many minute particulars, he had been able to concentrate the force of his mind on one perfect book and expound his views on the high subjects which occupied his thoughts in a systematic form. It cannot be maintained that Paul's Epistles are models of style. They were written far too hurriedly for this; and the last thing he thought of was to polish his periods. Often, indeed, his ideas, by the mere virtue of their fineness and beauty, run into forms of exquisite language, or there is in them such a sustained throb of emotion that they shape themselves spontaneously into sentences of noble eloquence. But oftener his language is rugged and formless; no doubt it was the first which came to hand for expressing what he had to say. He begins sentences and omits to finish them; he goes off into digressions and forgets to pick up the line of thought he has dropped; he throws out his ideas in lumps instead of fusing them into mutual coherence.

Nowhere perhaps will there be found so exact a parallel to the style of Paul as in the Letters and Speeches of Oliver Cromwell. In the Protector's brain there lay the best and truest thoughts about England and her complicated affairs which existed at the time in that island; but, when he tried to express them in speech or letter, there issued from his mind the most extraordinary mixture of exclamations, questions, arguments soon losing themselves in the sands of words, unwieldy parentheses, and morsels of beautiful pathos or subduing eloquence. Yet, as you read these amazing utterances, you come by degrees to feel that you are getting to see the very heart and soul of the Puritan Era, and that you would rather be beside this man than any other representative of the period. You see the events and ideas of the time in the very process of birth.

Perhaps, indeed, a certain formlessness is a natural accompaniment of the very highest originality. The perfect expression and orderly arrangement of ideas is a later process; but, when great thoughts are for the first time coming forth, there is a kind of primordial roughness about them, as if the earth out of which they are arising were still clinging to them: the polishing of the gold comes late and has to be preceded by the heaving of the ore out of the bowels of nature. Paul in his writings is hurling forth the original ore of truth. We owe to him hundreds of ideas which were never uttered before.

After the original man has got his idea out, the most commonplace scribe may be able to express it for others better than he, though he could never have originated it. So throughout the writings of Paul there are materials which others may combine into systems of theology and ethics, and it is the duty of the Church to do so. But his Epistles permit us to see revelation in the very process of birth. As we read them closely, we seem to be witnessing the creation of a world of truth, as the angels wondered to see the firmament evolving itself out of chaos and the multitudinous earth spreading itself forth in the light. Minute as are the details he has often to deal with, the whole of his vast view of the truth is recalled in his treatment of every one of them, as the whole sky is mirrored in a single drop of dew. What could be a more impressive proof of the fecundity of his mind than the fact that, amid the innumerable distractions of a second visit to his Greek converts, he should have written in half a year three such books as Romans, Galatians and Second Corinthians?

His Inspiration.—It was God by His Spirit who communicated this revelation of truth to Paul. Its own greatness and divineness supply the best proof that it could have had no other origin. But none the less did it break in upon Paul with the joy and pain of original thought; it came to him through his experience; it drenched and dyed every fiber of his mind and heart; and the expression which it found in his writings was in accordance with his peculiar genius and circumstances.

The Man Revealed in his Letters.—It would be easy to suggest compensations in the form of Paul's writings for the literary qualities they lack. But one of these so outweighs all others that it is sufficient by itself to justify in this case the ways of God. In no other literary form could we, to the same extent, in the writings have got the man. Letters are the most personal form of literature. A man may write a treatise or a history or even a poem and hide his personality behind it; but letters are valueless unless the writer shows himself. Paul is constantly visible in his letters. You can feel his heart throbbing in every chapter he ever wrote. He has painted his own portrait—not only that of the outward man, but of his innermost feelings—as no one else could have painted it. It is not from Luke, admirable as is the picture drawn in the Acts of the Apostles, that we learn what the true Paul was, but from Paul himself. The truths he reveals are all seen embodied in the man. As there are some preachers who are greater than their sermons, and the principal gain of their hearers, in listening to them, is obtained in the inspiring glimpses they obtain of a great and sanctified personality, so the best thing in the writings of Paul is Paul himself, or rather the grace of God in him.

CHAPTER SIX

Father, Where Art Thou?

This was the last time I saw my father alive in 2004.

Life after 9/11 was different. Even as people who knew me would smile, I knew deep down they had confused thoughts about my Muslim and Arabic background. While this huge matter was taking a toll on my life, I was also dealing with my wife, who wanted a divorce.

She was finished with our marriage. She filed for divorce and I thought my life was over. We had three children, a house, cars, and jobs. Life was going just fine. So what if we argued occasionally? And what if we were not infatuated with each other as we were in the early years? Despite friends telling us we were too young to marry, we did. Were we wrong?

Sixteen years after marrying, we divorced in 2001. I picked up the pieces and pressed on. The first few months were tough. But just like after any affliction, time healed the wounded heart, and the sky turned blue again. Birds started chirping after a silence of about a year. I was worried about our kids. Zade was nine and he suffered the most. It would take him a while to recover. Dury was five and while wanting Mommy and Daddy to be together, other things distracted him. Demi was one, and she never knew us as a couple. To her a broken family was the norm.

The kids would eventually recuperate. It is true that children are more resilient than adults. They did not mind having two Christmases and two sets of gifts. They also did not mind having two houses. When one parent was being tough, they could seek refuge with the other parent. My wife and I slowly figured out how to deal with each other. It is funny how after living with someone for sixteen years, you end up just fine living without them. God does miracles with our moxie. I was fine as long as my children were happy.

I would start "dating" again - I did not even know what that was. I was married at age twenty and had never dated much before marriage. It was like riding a bicycle, but for the first time and with training wheels. Things would be smooth for a while, then I would encounter a few bumps. I dated different women from all kinds of backgrounds. Some were believers and some were not. Faith was not high in my criteria, which included beauty, smarts, and sweetness. Conviction was way down the list. I was delighted to find a faithful woman who had other attributes I was attracted to, but I did not consider faith a *make-it-or-break-it* issue.

I went out with a Muslim, a Buddhist, a Christian, an agnostic, and others. I found myself mired in the midst of those beliefs, and I would start exploring different avenues to God. While dating the Buddhist, I studied Buddhism. From there, I ventured into Taoism, or the Tao Te Ching - a Chinese philosophy that advocates a simpler life and noninterference with natural things. I wanted a simpler life after my divorce. I was not inclined to believe in a rigid path like Christianity. I coveted what the Tao preached: Go with the flow. Swim with the current. Bend. The tree that stands against the wind will break.

Then I dated a Muslim and started reading the Quran again. She loved it and introduced me to her mosque, and I visited it several times. Except I found the same issues I had with Islam in my youth. So we broke up. I went solo for a while, and I felt Christ whispering for me to come back.

Dad

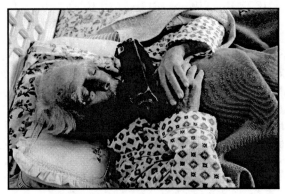

Dad slept with his radio blaring.

"Then I said to you, 'Do not be terrified; do not be afraid of them. The LORD your God, who is going before you, will fight for you, as he did for you in Egypt, before your very eyes, and in the desert. There you saw how the LORD your God carried you, as a father carries his son, all the way you went until you reached this place.'" Deuteronomy 1:29-31

I was sound asleep one early morning when I heard the phone buzzing. I reached for the nightstand where I normally put it to feel nothing. It kept on buzzing. Then I realized I had left it in the bathroom. "Ahhh, I will just return the call later," and went back to sleep.

Then I thought, "What if it is one of the kids? What if there was an emergency?" I pulled myself out of bed and walked in the bathroom to see our Syrian number on the screen. I breathed a sigh of relief. They always called at odd times.

"Karim?" my sister Mimi said.

"Hi Mimi . . . Yes. How are you?" I replied, detecting urgency in her voice.

"Its Dad, Karim. We have lost him. Dad is dead, Karim." Mimi said, crying.

My world turned black. I collapsed on the floor screaming: "No . . . No . . ."

Dad had been sick for a while. He had heart issues after his triple bypass surgery at age sixty, but made it to eighty-eight. I could hear Mimi shouting in the phone. But I let the phone drop on the cold floor and curled up next to it weeping. I would stay like that for about fifteen minutes until I nearly froze. I got up and wiped the tears and snot that had covered my face. I threw myself in bed and would not leave it for a couple of days. Friends filed in to check on me and bring me food. I did not eat and was pale and groggy. I managed to pull myself together after a few days and started proceedings to go to Syria.

Going home was not easy since I did not attend the mandatory military service. All Syrian youths are required to serve three years in the army after high school or college. I came to the Untied States and was not about to give three years of my life to something I did not believe in. I applied for a permit to return home through the embassy, which took three to four weeks. And while I waited, I missed the funeral of the man that was my whole world.

The first time it happened, I was shaving five days after Dad's death. Upon rinsing the razor, I heard my father say: *"Marhaba Karim."* (Hello Karim). I looked in the mirror and saw nothing, but I did hear him clear as a bell. I was a little shocked, but I attributed the voice to him being on my mind. I shook it off and went to work. It happened again in the car. The occurrence would repeat several times a day, and I started to have conversations with him. I thought I was going crazy, but at the same time I enjoyed it.

My papers finally came and I went home to see my mom and relatives at the airport all somber and subdued. We visited the gravesite the next day and I cried as I read his masthead: Kherridean Shamsi-Basha, 1917 – 2005. I looked at that hyphen in between the two dates and thought of the vast chasm interlaced. That tiny dash depicts everything we have done from birth to death. Our entire life is summarized with the smallest of lines. Dad was a writer who impacted many lives. Shouldn't there be a bigger line—one that endured for miles and miles?

A Flood of Memories

Dad was a lover of Arabic literature and published many books. He regarded poetry highly and spent most of his retirement in his library. He was honored during his last years as a poet and a writer.

Upon returning home from the cemetery, I visited with friends and relatives and ate way too much as I always do. The first night, Mimi made me a bed on the couch in the living room. It was the couch Dad took his nap on, and I could still smell him. I tried to go to sleep, but loving thoughts of my father kept me up. Certain attributes about this man were engraved in my brain. Some were as simple as peeling an apple, which he always did in one swoop. I would be watching and waiting, then he would cut the first piece and hand it over. I would take a bite and shake my head in approval. When the peel broke during the peeling process, we would laugh and I would say, "Aha, one point for me."

Some memories were of his surprises. I loved to go to his clothing store after school and torment Asghar, his Indian helper who seemed seventeen feet tall. The ironic thing was that Asghar means "smaller" in Arabic. This irony led my brother and me to make Asghar's life miserable. We set booby traps that he would repeatedly fall for. The one he fell for every time was placing a bucket of water atop the cracked door of the storage room, which he entered a hundred times a day. He would be drenched time after time. Another favorite was stretching a rope at ankle height across the hallway and waiting for him to walk by and fall. We put salt instead of sugar in his coffee, and cough syrup in his cokes.

scoundrel would have boxed your ears

Poor Asghar, he would chase us out of the store and Dad would smile while telling us to behave.

One day Asghar was not at the store and there was no one to booby trap. I was trying to do my math homework without a calculator like the teacher unfairly requested. "What does he know?" I thought, "You can do math a lot quicker with a calculator." And there it was taunting me at the shop next door: a black beauty with yellow buttons that could add, subtract, multiply, and divide. It cost three dinars so Dad said it had to wait. I was fuming, "This math homework would be finished if I had the calculator." I would look at other kids and hate them, "I bet they all have calculators."

Dad said he was going out for a while. I didn't care. I normally went with him, but today, he was not on my favorite list. Dad returned and laid a brown paper bag in front of me. I opened it thinking it was a snack but found the black and yellow machine. I didn't know where the heavenly spotlight came from, or the opera singing, but I smiled from ear to ear and started on the road to becoming a math genius. I would never rival Einstein, but my homework did get an A that day. And it took a lot less time . . . teachers!

I was the only one who got away with everything.

Dad and I would discuss religion for hours. He would encourage me to read and discover. I was exhausted with that word. "How can you discover religion?" I would ask. "Aren't you born into it? Why would you discover it later?" One day he took me to the balcony of our condo bountiful with big and fat red geraniums that filled the air with a sweet smell. He spent hours tending to those geraniums, and it showed. They were fragrant and huge. Our neighbors would ask him for his secret. He would smile and say, "Lots of love." He plucked a flower and handed it to me. He then asked me to stretch out my arm and close my eyes.

"What?" I said. He insisted, so I did, hoping no one could see me acting like an idiot, especially the girls on the second floor of the building facing ours. I had spent a great deal of time working hard to get one of them to smile, and now she was expecting the next move. I did not want her to see me being a poetic flower lover.

Dad said to bring my hand slowly to my nose and inhale at the same time, then to stop when I could smell it. I did. I started bending my arm and inhaling, thinking this couldn't take long. It seemed like minutes before the smell finally hit me and flooded all of my senses. I opened my eyes screaming, "I smell it, I smell it!" Dad looked at me calmly and said, "Discovering is like the smell" – and he walked away. I stood there stunned, looking at the geranium in my hand.

Dad's desk hid many of his favorite things.

I got up the next morning and went to his ancient desk. It was a gigantic wooden desk that had seen better days, and it was packed with treasures. It smelled like relics from the Ottoman Empire were hidden in its midst. Dad never threw anything away. There were little pieces of paper, erasers, pencil sharpeners, pens, rubber bands, typewriter ribbons, tiny tools, small toys, little books, and tens of notebooks. I came across a box of old diaries. I pulled the one from 1965, the year I was born, and opened to my birthday to find out he had been in Europe on a buying trip:

"Today Lila delivered our fourth child. I was so happy and called her immediately from Italy after the Telegram. She said she did not know what to name him. She put Farress (Knight) on the birth certificate. I told her to name him Karim. My Dad's name was Abdul Karim. Karim is one of the Muslim names for God, and we are supposed to put Abdul before it, which means 'slave of.' I do not want my son to be a slave even to God. So I named him Karim without Abdul." Wow, I knew that was how he felt, but not strong enough to write it in a diary. That explains a lot about my father. He was a proud man. Little did my father know that his decision would bring me grief in school as I was told a million times that my name should have been Abdul Karim.

While rummaging through the ancient desk, the same desk that Dad allowed me to sit on when little and make a mess of his papers and pens, I found an old photo album from a trip we took to Kuwait one year. My siblings and I covered the backseat of the giant Plymouth with a mattress, transforming it into a playground. Then we added pillows and blankets and toys and balls that would help pass the time while traveling the dessert of Southeast Syria, Iraq, and Kuwait. The trip would take two days. We played games and fought while Dad drove, and Mom fed everyone. She prepared an icebox filled with food and a gigantic block of ice that would remain solid two long and hot days. One of the photographs I found was of my brother and me in front of the car. I closed my eyes and smiled.

*My brother and me on our giant car
during the trip through the Iraqi Desert.*

During a long and a hot part of that trip, we were asleep in the backseat when a loud pop woke everyone up. The car started to swerve to the right, and all of us in the back slammed into the left side on top of each other. My sisters were screaming, my brother was screaming, and I was on the bottom trying not to suffocate. Then the car swerved to the left, and I ended up on top of everyone, crashing into the right side. This happened a few times. I remember looking at Dad calmly trying to tame the angry monster. His sleeves were rolled up, and his sweaty arms looked gargantuan as he maneuvered the out-of-control car to a stop.

We had a flat tire in the middle of the hot and dry Iraqi Desert. Dad replaced it with the spare and we spent the night in the small town of Basra. The room we rented was full of giant roaches, so the four of us kids decided to sleep in the car. My two sisters slept inside the car. My brother and I slept on a blanket on top. It was a clear and cold night full of bright stars, just like that night in the Boy Scout campout. We stayed up talking. Maher believed in God and had explanations for this vast universe that did not satisfy me. "God made everything, you just have to believe that," he said.

"How can He make these hundreds and hundreds of stars and planets? Out of what? Can't be out of nothing?" I would say.

"You are going to get in trouble talking like that ya Fasfoos." He always called me Fasfoos (Stinker).

"But why can't no one explain things?"

"Shut up and go to sleep," Maher said.

I laid on the car with only my eyes showing from under the blanket so the flying roaches wouldn't land on me. I stared at the sky, then I looked at the horizon to see the natural gas smokestacks bright across the far dessert night. The luminosity of the smokestacks emitting blue flames contrasted with the brilliance of the stars above. "I guess if man can make things burn and give light, God can as well." And I faded to sleep.

Maher also could tell me anything and I would believe him. Like the day he was tired of fighting with Mom and decided to run away from home and take me with him. I refused, until he said, "There is no school where I am going." I hated school, and that was enough to sway an eight-year-old brain. We packed our backpacks with clothes and chocolate and water bottles, and started to walk down the street. After about half an hour of silence, I asked, "Where are we going?"

"I don't know. Shut up," Maher said.

I started to cry as I sensed his nervousness. He told me to hush and keep walking. I sat on the sidewalk and refrained from going any further, when a car that looked familiar crept up. It was Dad. I screamed and hugged him tight. He took us for ice cream and not a word was ever spoken about the failed runaway attempt.

I finished my search for treasures and filled a box I would bring back to the States. When I miss Dad, I look in the box and find a treasure every time.

The Memory of All Memories

Perhaps the most memorable event with my father took place the year I saw him last. He called me into the library, which by itself was a huge happening. He did not waste time speaking to anyone during his last days, he just hibernated with his books. Upon entering the library, he ushered me to sit down, looked at me with love, and said, "I have read some of the Bible, and I want to ask you a few questions."

I was shocked. Up to this point, I had never said anything

about converting to Christianity. "Did he know?" I swallowed and shook my head.

He continued to bring up all kinds of contradictions between *what?* the Old Testament and the New Testament. He also pointed out some prophecies that in his opinion proved the Bible to be fabricated.

I responded by pointing out the Old Testament was finished four hundred years before the New Testament, and I showed him some prophecies that could not be fabricated. He was impressed with Psalm 22 and Isaiah 53. After the three-hour discussion, he concluded that the Quran has just as many if not more contradictions, and that the Bible might be correct in some sense. Mom called us for lunch and the talk was over.

The next morning he buzzed me to come into the library again. I went in as he smiled and said, "You won't believe the dream I had last night." Then he proceeded to tell me:

"I was at an oasis in the desert, and all these people came and started speaking with their own languages. There must have been over a hundred tongues. But you know what? They all understood each other. It was windy, and there was fire, it was amazing." Then he reclined back in his chair.

I was delighted. I replied, "Dad, your dream is from the Bible, can I show you?" I flipped the Arabic Bible he had to the second chapter of Acts and the Pentecost story:

"When the day of Pentecost came, they were all together in one place. Suddenly a sound like the blowing of a violent wind came from heaven and filled the whole house where they were sitting. They saw what seemed to be tongues of fire that separated and came to rest on each of them. All of them were filled with the Holy Spirit and began to speak in other tongues as the Spirit enabled them. Now there were staying in Jerusalem God-fearing Jews from every nation under heaven. When they heard this sound, a crowd came together in bewilderment, because each one heard their own language being spoken. Utterly amazed, they asked: 'Aren't all these who are speaking Galileans? Then how is it that each of us hears them in our native language? Parthians, Medes and Elamites; residents of Mesopotamia, Judea and Cappadocia, Pontus and Asia, Phrygia and Pamphylia, Egypt and the parts of Libya near Cyrene; visitors from Rome (both Jews and converts to Judaism); Cretans and Arabs—we hear them

declaring the wonders of God in our own tongues!' Amazed and perplexed,
they asked one another, 'What does this mean?'" Acts 2:1-11

He stopped me there and said, "This is exactly my dream.
What does it mean?"

I said, "Hold on," and I continued reading:

"Then Peter stood up with the Eleven, raised his voice and addressed the
crowd: 'Fellow Jews and all of you who live in Jerusalem, let me explain
this to you; listen carefully to what I say. These people are not drunk, as
you suppose. It's only nine in the morning! No, this is what was spoken by
the prophet Joel: "In the last days, God says, I will pour out my Spirit on
all people. Your sons and daughters will prophesy, your young men will see
visions, your old men will dream dreams.""" Acts 2:14-17

I stopped and looked at him. His mouth was open, and his
eyes were huge. I smiled and said, "You must have read that part
and it stuck with you."

"I never read 'A'mal Arrasool' *(The Book of Acts),*" he said
with a low voice, then added, "Can you give me some time to
digest this?"

"Sure" I replied and left him staring at the Bible. He spent the
next few hours in the library, went for a walk, and went to bed
without talking to anyone. I figured he just needed space.

The next day he went about his usual business. I asked him
what he thought, and he said he will be thinking about it for a
while and will let me know. The subject never came up again,
but he was at peace. I kept seeing the Bible being carried from
the bedroom where he read at night, to the library during the day.

I came back to the States, and we never visited the dream
again. I don't know to what extent it had affected Dad. He died
less than a year later.

A Double Dose of Deity

"Though I am free and belong to no one, I have made myself a slave to
everyone, to win as many as possible. To the Jews I became like a Jew,
to win the Jews. To those under the law I became like one under the law

(though I myself am not under the law), so as to win those under the law. To those not having the law I became like one not having the law (though I am not free from God's law but am under Christ's law), so as to win those not having the law. To the weak I became weak, to win the weak. I have become all things to all people so that by all possible means I might save some." 1 Corinthians 9:19-22

I came back to the United States and felt lost and confused. I became both Christian and Muslim. When people asked me what I was, they would look at me with a bewildered face. It worked for me. I wanted Christianity with its forgiveness, grace, and love. But I also wanted Islam, the religion my father was proud for me to have. I felt divided and unsettled, but it was the only thing I could do. The divorce in 2001 was a monster, and losing Dad in 2005 was another monster. I was mad at God, whoever He was.

I floated on a rickety raft in a sea of religions in 2006 and 2007. Actually, religion was the last thing on my mind. I started to enjoy dating and living the single life. I settled into a routine of comfort. Life as a commitment-phobic man regarding faith and women can be very satisfying. Taking a stand was far from my intentions. I went with the flow. I was the tree that bent every time a storm passed.

Then God put a woman in my path that would harden my stand against the blistering winds of rejecting Him.

Your Journey

"So now faith, hope, and love abide, these three; but the greatest of these is love." 1 Corinthians 13:13

_____

_____

_____

_____

_____

_____

_____

_____

_____

_____

_____

_____

_____

_____

_____

_____

_____

Surrender and Consecration
by Benjamin B. Warfield

When Paul was stricken to the ground on his way to Damascus by the glory of the risen Christ, bursting on him from heaven, he had but two questions to ask: "Who art thou, Lord?" and "What shall I do, Lord?" By the first he certified himself as to the person before whose majesty he lay prone; by the second he entered at once into His willing service.

In this, too, Paul's conversion is typical. No one can call Jesus Lord save by the Holy Ghost; but when the Holy Ghost has moved with power upon the soul, the amazed soul has but two questions to ask: "Who art thou, Lord?" and "What shall I do, Lord?" There is no question in its mind as to the legitimacy of the authority claimed, as to its extent and limitations, as to its sphere, as to its sanction. He whose glory has shone into the heart is recognized at once and unquestioningly as Lord, and is so addressed no less in the first question than in the second. "Who art thou, Lord?" is not a demand for credentials; it is a simple inquiry for information, a cry of wondering adoration and worship. And it is, therefore, followed at once with the cry of, "What shall I do, Lord?"

In this latter question there unite the two essential elements of all religion, *surrender and consecration*—the passive and active aspects of that faith which on the human side is the fundamental element of religion, as grace is on God's side, when dealing with sinful men. "What shall I do, Lord?" In that simple question, as it trembled on the lips of Paul lying prostrate in the presence of the heavenly glory, there pulsated all that abnegation of self, that casting of oneself wholly on Christ, that firm entrusting of oneself in all the future to Him and His guidance,—in a word, the whole of saving faith. And saving faith wherever found is sure to take this position, perhaps not purely—for what faith of man is absolutely pure?—but in direct proportion to its purity, its governing power over the life. *Surrender and consecration*, we may take it then, are the twin key-notes of the Christian life, "What shall I do, Lord?" the one question which echoes through all the corridors of the Christian heart.

And now let us observe what is involved in such a spirit. I think we may say this much on even a surface survey of the matter—(1) that there is an element of *humility* that enters into it; (2) that there is an element of *true dignity* that enters into it, and (3) that there is *an element of power* that enters into it. Humility, dignity, power— at least these three things.

Humility—what a difference in this regard between Saul the Pharisee and Paul the Christian! Before his conversion Saul seems to have had no doubt of what he should do. His fundamental characteristics seem to have been those of the type of character which we call masterful. He was a man of decision, of energy; somewhat self-sufficient, as indeed a Pharisaic training was apt to make one; little inclined, one would think, to defer to the guidance of others. We must guard against supposing him to have been a man of violent and wicked impulses, as we may be misled into fancying by his career as a persecutor and his own words of subsequent sharp self-rebuke—after his eyes were opened. A man of deep religious heart at all times, set on serving the Lord, his very vices were but the defects of his virtues. But somewhat headstrong, opinionated, undocile, perhaps; bent on serving God with a pure conscience, but constitutionally apt to go his own way in that service—for the God of Israel had never bidden him persecute the saints, and that was an outgrowth, we may be sure, of his habitual self-direction. What can I do to glorify the God of Israel—we may be sure that he had often asked himself that very question—nay, that it was always echoing through his soul and was the lode-star of all his life. There was nothing small or little in Paul's Pharisaic life; no reserves in his devotion to his ideal, and no shrinking from labor, or difficulty, or danger. Paul never was a place-seeker, never was a sycophant, never was self-indulgent, or self-sparing. The elements of a great character wrought in him mightily. What he lacked was not readiness to do and dare; what he lacked was humility. And the change that took place in him on the road to Damascus was in this regard no less immense than immediate. It was a totally new note which vibrated through his being, that found expression in the humble inquiry, "What shall I do, Lord?" It is no longer a question directed to himself, "What shall *I* do?—what shall *I*, in my learning and strength and devotion—what shall *I* do to the glory of God?" It is the final and utter renunciation of self and the subjection of the whole life to the guidance of another.

"What shall I do, *Lord*?" Heretofore Paul had been, even in his service to God, self-led; hereafter he was to be, even in the common affairs of life, down to his eating and drinking, God-led. It is the characteristic change that makes the Christian; for the Christian is particularly the Spirit-led man: they that are led by the Spirit of God, they are the sons of God. And as the Christian more and more perfectly assumes the attitude of a constant and unreserved "What shall I do, Lord?", he more and more perfectly enters into his Christian heritage, and lives out his Christian life—the very keynote of which is thus easily seen to be humility.

Dignity—there is an element of dignity which enters into this attitude also. For humility is not to be mistaken for a degrading supineness. Lowliness of mind is far from being the same with lowness of mind. When Paul ceased to be self-led and became Christ-led, he did not by that step become low in mind or morals; it was a step upwards, and not downwards. There is a lurking feeling in most of us, no doubt, that our dignity consists just in our self-government. Self-sufficiency is its note, or, as we perhaps prefer to call it, self-dependence. That man is really a man, we are prone to think, who carves out his own fortune, rests on his own efforts, and seeks favor and certainly direction from no one. Now there is a proper basis for this feeling; we need courageous men who call no man master and swear in the words of none; this self-centred, self-poised, and independent nature is one of the best gifts of God—cultivate it! But it is very easy for a proper self-pride and a high-minded independence to pass into a very improper self-sufficiency. We were not intended to defer with servile incapacity to any fellow-creature's direction; but there is a place for authority in the world after all; and as liberty must not be allowed to lapse into license, so independence must not be permitted to degenerate into self-assertion. God did not create mankind atomistically but as a race; and it is the part of true dignity to find our true relations and to subject ourselves to them. It is not a mark of manhood to separate ourselves from the bands that unite mankind into an organism, but to take each his place in the organism and thoroughly to fill it.

He who hitches his chariot to a star is not thereby sinking to a lower status. True as this is in worldly matters it is superlatively true in spiritual affairs. The man led by the Spirit of God—the Christ-led man—is the man of highest, and not of lowest, dignity. As it is the mark of a Christian man that he is "under orders," so it is the source of all his dignity that he is "under orders."

What is the primary characteristic of Christendom but just this,—that God has taken charge of it, given it His orders, a revelation we call it; while heathendom is without this book of general orders. And what is the characteristic of the Christian man but just this: that he has found his Captain and receives his orders from Him? "What shall I do, Lord?"— that is the note of his life. And is it not clear that it is the source of an added dignity and worth to his life? Just as the soldier is nothing but the hoodlum licked into shape by coming under orders— under the establishing and forming influence of legitimate and wise authority—so the Christian is nothing but the sinner, come under the formative influence of the Captain of us all.

Power—it lies in the very nature of the case that such a coming under orders is the source of a vast increase also of power. For it is at once to find our place in a great and powerful organism. So the soldier finds it, though this is not the primary fact of his betterment which he perceives as a result of his coming under orders. That, as Kipling rightly sees, is the subjective effect on himself, the increase of self-respect and of general dignity and conscious worth which comes to him. But the increase of power also is a factor of high moment. A cog wheel is a useless piece of iron by itself; but in its legitimate place in the machine it works wonders. An individual is as nothing in this seething mass of humanity which we call the world; be he never so energetic he can work no effect, but all his activity is like the aimless dashing of a moth about the destroying flame. But let him find his true place in the organism of humanity, and the weakest of us becomes a factor in the inevitable rush of the whole towards its destined end. See, then, the element of power in the question, "What shall I do, Lord?" For we must keep fully in mind that this human race of which we are members is not simply a chance aggregation of individuals, like a mass of worms crawling restlessly this way and that as the native impulse of each directs. It cannot be atomistically conceived. It is an organism, in which each individual has his appointed place and function. It is not merely the dictate of wisdom but the condition of efficiency and power that we should each find this, our place, and fulfill our own function.

If sin had never entered the world, this would doubtless be an easy task; we should each fit well into the place in which we find ourselves and should fulfill our required functions smoothly and easily, and each in his appointed measure advance the race to its destined goal. But sin has spoiled all; and the disjointed mechanism lies broken and dismantled and unable to work at its task. It is, therefore, that Christ Jesus has come into the world, the head of a new humanity, for the restoration of the race to its harmony with itself, the universe, and its appointed work. It is only through Him and through His direction as the Captain of our salvation that we may discover or occupy our place in His Church, which is only another name for reorganized humanity. Therefore the noble figure of Paul, which compares the Church to a body and us to members in particular. How shall the members of a body act? Each going his own way, independently of and inconsiderately of the others? Where then would be the body? But how find our true place and task in this organism of the body of Christ? There can be but one way and that way is pointed to by Paul's question, "What shall I do, Lord?" He and He only can appoint to their functions the members of His body, and thus the way of continued humility and dignity is easily seen to be also the way of power.

Brethren that is the way we are to conquer the world; and our part in it is just to obey orders. "What shall I do, Lord?" is to be our one question, and simple obedience to the response our one duty. Ah, in all our life, if we value success—the success of Christ—let us make Paul's question the one single, simple matter of our lives. Let "Lord, what shall I do?" be our sole chart for all the journey of life.

CHAPTER SEVEN

Is Jesus Christ Your Lord and Savior?

Dana at the mountains of Colorado

"We put no obstacle in anyone's way, so that no fault may be found with our ministry, but as servants of God we commend ourselves in every way: by great endurance, in afflictions, hardships, calamities, beatings, imprisonments, riots, labors, sleepless nights, hunger; by purity, knowledge, patience, kindness, the Holy Spirit, genuine love; by truthful speech, and the power of God; with the weapons of righteousness for the right hand and for the left; through honor and dishonor, through slander and praise. We are treated as impostors, and yet are true; as unknown, and yet well known; as dying, and behold, we live; as punished, and yet not killed; as sorrowful, yet always rejoicing; as poor, yet making many rich; as having nothing, yet possessing everything." 2 Corinthians 6:3-10

I had given up on dating by the summer of 2008. I was totally satisfied alone and focused on my kids, when out of nowhere I met Dana. Unknown to me, she would turn my faith life right side up. We connected immediately. Her grandfather had come from

Lebanon to America in 1912 and raised his family here, basking in opportunity and freedom. She was raised American for the most part, but longed to date someone who knew the Arabic language, food, and culture. She was a beauty with long black hair and hazel eyes the color of honey. Her voice was sweet and so was her demeanor. When she smiled, you had no choice but to smile back.

Dana and I talked on the telephone for a week, then we met and from the beginning, we were crazy about each other. The next weekend she would come to Birmingham to visit me before traveling to Colorado like she did every summer. Her three kids were already there. They were similar ages to my children. She was a strong believer in Christ and wanted to make sure I was as well. Since late 2007, I had been slowly coming back to Christianity. The few years I spent as a Universalist after the death of my father ended and I would seek Jesus again, but still on my terms, and still without considering Him my Savior. I was not about to be saved alone without my family.

Dana called me from Colorado one evening. After small talk, she asked me a question that raised the hair on the back of my neck, "You say you are a Christian, but is Jesus Christ your Lord and Savior?"

I thought to myself, "There are those words again. Why do people even say them? And why do I have to declare him as such?"

"I am for sure a Christian, but I do not do those words," I said with an irritated voice.

Dana was not the kind of woman who sugarcoated things. She replied, "You can't be a Christian if you don't 'do' those words, Karim."

"How dare you tell me what I am and what I am not?" I said. "I am a Christian, and I don't care if you believe me."

She tried to calm me down but it was too late. I had already started down a one-way road leading to that small castle I had constructed with a moat around it. The castle that shielded me from admitting my daily fall, and the castle that replaced redemption and the need for a Savior with my own version of Christianity: where no one needed to be saved.

I hung up mad and started to slam doors and hit walls. "I

cannot believe she questioned my Christianity. The nerve of that woman."

I laid in bed after I calmed down a bit but could not sleep. I kept thinking of this nonending dilemma. Will I ever find peace?

I finally dozed off only to wake up a few times soaking wet. I had weird dreams. It was one of the worst nights of my life. I was hot despite the air conditioner humming all night, and my hand hurt from punching the wall. Early in the morning, the phone rang and it was Dana.

I had written her off. "She is not going to date a man with my thinking. Fine if she wants a narrow-minded person like herself," I thought.

Dana had gone for a hike and thought about our conversation the night before. She finally decided to call me from the top of a rock where she felt the closest to God.

I reluctantly answered the phone. "Karim, how are you?" Dana asked.

"Fine," I replied.

"I may have a solution for your problem," she added.

I chuckled. For the past twelve years since my near-conversion in 1996, I had been on a serious search for a solution to the *Savior* predicament. I have talked to many pastors and theologians, and none of them were able to resolve the problem to my satisfaction. Even Gil, the pastor who baptized me, told me that God would deal with my issues after I made the leap. Well, I made the leap, but God was still silent.

"You do, don't you? Well please share it with me," I said with a sarcastic tone.

Dana ignored my acrimony and continued, "I know you are concerned about your family. Your family is in the hands of God; what about just Karim and Jesus?"

For a few seconds, I looked at the phone to make sure I heard her right. "Can you repeat that?" I said.

"I said your family is in the hands of God. What if it was only Jesus and you? Would He be your Lord and Savior?"

I could sense her words falling onto the depth of my soul. I paused a few seconds, weighing those words. A certain peace fell upon me that I could not explain. Right before she asked me that question, I felt uneasy and almost angry. After the question, I felt a peace that surpassed my understanding. I calmly said,

"If it is just Jesus and me, well . . . he is my everything, Dana. He can be my Lord and Savior . . . But . . ." I wanted to question her about my family.

She interrupted me, saying, "There is no 'but' Karim. You just became a Christian."

I started crying, and she started crying. I had been sitting on the edge of my bed, but I got up and started pacing the floor with elation. I was in disbelief. How can a woman I met two weeks before solve a twelve-year-old battle with one phone call?

I hung up the phone and smiled while crying. "Is He really my Lord and Savior?" Is it just He and I? I can call him that. He is finally my Lord and Savior. But what does that mean? I guess Lord means He will be the master when it comes to decisions. I need to give things up to His will. I thought of Psalm 23, which I have become a fan of, joining millions of people who consider this Psalm dear and intimate:

"The Lord is my shepherd; I shall not want.
He makes me lie down in green pastures.
He leads me beside still waters.
He restores my soul.
He leads me in paths of righteousness for his name's sake.

Even though I walk through the valley of the shadow of death, I will fear
no evil, for you are with me;
your rod and your staff, they comfort me.
You prepare a table before me in the presence of my enemies;
you anoint my head with oil;
my cup overflows.
Surely goodness and mercy shall follow me all the days of my life,
and I shall dwell in the house of the Lord forever."

According to this Psalm, He is my Lord; at the same time, He is the humblest of people. He is my Shepherd. I liked the dichotomy.

Something else Dana said sounded familiar, "My family is in the hands of God."

I couldn't place where I had heard that statement before. Someone had said it to me years and years ago. Then I remembered. It was Rev. Frank Barker, the narrow-minded preacher who said, "Your family is in the hands of God. What are you going to do?" The words did not register with me at the time. But now, those words meant the whole world. Where is Rev. Frank Barker now?

I began to ponder many questions: "So if Jesus is now my Savior…Wow…How could I have been a Christian without a Savior? What about my repeated sin that I do daily? How was I going to redeem that sin? I could not believe I lived for twelve years without redemption. I have so much to make right. Or, I guess I don't, because God wipes the slate clean every time we confess our sins. Redemption comes with confession, because Jesus Christ is the Savior who shed his blood for my sins and the sins of this world. This is quite unbelievable. The eminence and grandeur of the idea alone cannot belong to a human. Humans have thought of countless ways to redeem their sin through animal sacrifice and worshiping other gods. Only Jesus gave Himself up, and by the virtue of believing in Him alone, one is forgiven. There is no way man came up with this idea. It must be of God."

Something else I came to realize – I felt as if I had been given a new heart:

"And I will give you a new heart, and a new spirit I will put within you. And I will remove the heart of stone from your flesh and give you a heart of flesh." Ezekiel 36:26

This new heart would love God instead of fear Him; it would be in fellowship with Him as He dwelt in me. Wow! "Dwelt in me?" That will take some getting used to! I also placed my complete trust in the Lord for the first time. Awareness of trusting him alone was also new.

Not So Fast

Dana was sitting on her rock in the beautiful mountains of Colorado. While she was on the phone with me, her son had been riding his bike down the mountain when a deer jumped in front of him. He slammed into the animal and flew off the bike, landing on his arm and shoulder. He ended up at the emergency room with stitches all over his arm. Dana rushed to the hospital. She would remember that day as not only the day I came to Salvation, but also a day when satan tried to distract her from leading me to that Salvation.

We dated for three years and delved into the Word together. We read devotionals and shared Scripture every day. She was everything I wanted in a woman. And now that faith was high on my criteria, Dana met my entire list, and I met hers. She introduced me to parts of the Bible I had never read before, like the books of Daniel, Esther, and Revelation. I loved Daniel and the stand he took. I adored Esther and the tenacity she had. And I dived into Revelation and the visions it contains. My faith journey became stronger as I got into the Word, and as I shared what I found with Dana. That woman is responsible for teaching me the importance of reading the Word daily.

The Secret

Scripture started to take on a new meaning. I would find verses that would cast a profound impact on me. Verses like John 15:7: *"If you abide in me, and my words abide in you, ask whatever you wish, and it will be done for you."*

It was a year after the book *The Secret* became a best seller. It ascribed the idea of attaining what you believed to philosophers, sages, professors, and thinkers. I would find the true *secret* all over the Bible. The idea of achieving what your faith leads you to believe belonged to God way before the contemplation of man. There is still one condition - it has to be God's *will* for it to happen.

And you have to be obediant for faith to deeply root itself in your life. Faith without obedience cannot exist.

I collected about eighty verses with that meaning: *If you have faith and believe you can attain something, it will be yours.* I also knew it was not automatic. You still have to pray and be obedient and work hard and set goals and take the steps necessary. And you still have to submit to His will. But faith is vital.

I also discovered a whole new meaning to the verse that kept me away from believing in Christ for a long time:

"Jesus said to him, 'I am the way, and the truth, and the life. No one comes to the Father except through me.'" John 14:6

I finally believed the essence of that verse. It was all about Jesus and me. My burden for my family still existed, and I will pray that one day they can be believers in Christ as well. And my dead father? I am just willing to trust that through some unexplainable event, he met Christ on his way home. No matter, I grew into peace with Salvation, and Jesus Christ became my *Lord* and *Savior*.

I finally told my family that I had converted from Islam to Christianity. Mom screamed on the phone and started lecturing me that I CAN NOT and WILL NOT convert. That I would go straight to hell if I did. My sister Mimi just about fainted. I just told them that I loved them and that God loved them. Mom kept lecturing, "What would your dad say if he was still alive?" I responded, "But Mom, I now have a Heavenly Father who is always with me, it is wonderful." She started crying and Mimi was crying. "*Haram alaik*," (It is forbidden) Mom kept saying while crying. That phone call ended, and despite the animosity, I felt the weight of the world lifted off my shoulders.

I knew the great pain they were going through. I also knew that I couldn't live hiding His light any longer. The burden I endured for years, while being a Christian who denied his faith in front of his family, vanished. And with Facebook all over the Arab world, my extended family knows, and for the most part they have accepted the fact. One time, a cousin lectured me about leaving

Islam, and another cousin reprimanded him. My sister Rowaida in New York does not bring it up. I am just letting them see the light of Christ in me. And if the subject comes up, I would be happy to discuss it. I hope one day I can go to Syria and share God's love with my whole family.

They'll lop off his head!

My Children

My three children (from left) Dury, Zade, and Demi

My fatherhood took on a whole new meaning. I started to see Christ in my children and through them. My awareness of their actions would create a vivid canvas I painted with a bright brush. Like the night Zade inducted me into the "Father-of-a-Teenager Hall of Fame."

Zade played his trumpet for the first time with the Homewood High School Marching Band. I arrived at the stadium with the glee of a new papa and immediately looked for him among the sea of Homewood Patriots in the stands to no avail. So I waited until the halftime show hoping to catch a glimpse of him on the field.

When the band started marching, I realized that spotting Zade was going to be harder than I had imagined. After straining my eyes and following a line of trumpeters, I saw him. I wanted to point to him and scream, "This is my boy!" But they ran to start a new song, and I lost him again.

After the show, I wanted Zade to see me. His cousin dragged me by the hand to the stage facing the band. I was standing next to the drum major facing three hundred high schoolers. I felt all of them looking at me as if I were a guest conductor. She pointed to Zade and I saw him. My face lit up, and I forgot that I was extremely obvious. I waved a fast wave. He had warned me in the past about my wave. He said, "Dad, you don't wave like THAT. You don't raise your hand and wiggle your fingers. Just raise the hand and put it down quickly."

Zade looked at me with a blank stare, then he mouthed two words deliberately and precisely. I looked at his cousin who said, "I think he said, 'GO AWAY.'" I nodded in agreement, smiled, and quietly walked off the stage.

I will forever cherish that moment with my oldest son, and other moments with Dury and Demi. Like the day Dury told me not to look at him while I was picking him up from school. Or the day Demi saw me in her band room and made a 180-degree turn and walked away. I laugh at such events and consider them part of God's plan, that my children would go through the teenage years with its unexplainable behavior, but then grow to be faithful people who love God. My kids would become good friends with Dana's kids, and they would constantly make fun of Dana and me. We took it well and despite the occasional misunderstanding, things went as well as they could.

Dana and I were engaged to marry until the crash in the economy made my work dwindle. I had a hard time continuing to date Dana while supporting my children. The economic decline finally took its toll on both of us and we sadly broke up. I loved Dana like I loved no one before. It was the love I was supposed to grow in: where God comes first, then your partner and children. I had never even considered loving God more than my wife or my children, but that is truly a love so amazing. Even love like that can languish with hardship and no resources. My work suffered to the point that I had to sell my house. I moved in with a friend since I couldn't afford an apartment, and I tried hard to revive my photography. I was having a hard time making ends meet.

Homeless ... Really?

This is where I parked my car during my week of sleeping in the coffee shop parking lot.

"We are fools for Christ, but you are so wise in Christ! We are weak, but you are strong! You are honored, we are dishonored! To this very hour we go hungry and thirsty, we are in rags, we are brutally treated, we are homeless. We work hard with our own hands. When we are cursed, we bless; when we are persecuted, we endure it; when we are slandered, we answer kindly. We have become the scum of the earth, the garbage of the world—right up to this moment." 1 Corinthians 4:10-13

I stayed with friends for about a year, spending a month here and two weeks there. Then there was a week where no one could take me, so I spent the night in my car in the parking lot of a coffee shop. I was officially homeless. I never lost sight of God and could feel Him close by. Although I was at a loss of why He was allowing my austerity.

"Come on God, throw me a bone please," I would pray. He did throw me several bones. Every time I would have a pressing bill, I would receive a call for a job. I still accumulated a good deal of debt. But nothing humbled me like the week in the parking lot. It opened my eyes and heart to all the homeless out there. My stint was short and manageable, even though it was during a freezing January.

On the first night, I parked the car behind the coffee shop after it closed at ten o'clock and cranked on the heater for a few minutes. Then I turned the car off and covered up with a blanket and went to sleep. I did not know that the restaurants surrounding the coffee shop would take their garbage out to the dumpster next to the car. Not wanting them to see me and call the police, I sunk in my seat and covered up. Finally around two in the morning, there was no more garbage to dump. Except the temperature had dipped below freezing and I had to start the car for a few minutes every hour to get some heat. I slept for a few hours and woke up to the sanitation truck emptying the dumpster. I washed up in the bathroom of the coffee shop and started my day.

Sleeping in my car would become customary. One day I was on my way to Nashville to pick up a few items from a friend, when my twenty-year-old car decided to quit. I towed it to a mechanic who wanted four hundred dollars for a new fuel pump. I barely had the money. "We will put it in first thing in the morning," the man said.

"In the morning? What about now?" I said.

"We're closing in fifteen minutes, buddy. It takes hours to put on a fuel pump. Mo'ning buddy," he replied.

That night, I did what I had become a pro at: leaned my car seat back, covered up with a blanket, and went to sleep in the shop parking lot. Shortly after I dozed off, I was awakened by a clanging noise. I opened my eyes to see a drifter walking with a grocery store cart full of aluminum cans. I turned and shut my eyes. I wondered what his story was and how long he had been homeless. Next thing I know there was a loud thud on the back of the car. I jumped and looked back to see two guys leaning against my car talking. I could barely hear what they were saying, so I cracked the window open.

"I told you there ain't no women at that bar, you're an idiot," said one of them.

"What about that smokin' waitress?" said the other.

"Yeah, she was smokin' alright. Now shut up and get me a Coke."

They moved to the drink machine near the door of the mechanic shop and fiddled with change while kicking the machine. One of them started throwing rocks and yelling. I sunk in my seat further. It was about midnight, and there were no police cars anywhere close. They came back and sat on the front hood of my car smoking. I was terrified. I was in the little town of Pulaski, Tennessee, where the Ku Klux Klan was born. They talked and smoked for a while, and finally got off the car and walked away. I was relieved. I tried to get back to sleep. It was almost one in the morning. I dozed off a few hours, then got my car repaired and moved on.

To say that any leftover pride was annihilated would be an understatement. I did have some pride issues. It is not easy to forgo something you were raised eating and drinking and breathing. But after becoming a believer, I did learn to walk that fine line between humility and pride. It was a line that morphed into whatever you were experiencing at the time. You were humble for the most part. If you needed to have a little pride in your work as an artist, you humbly stood up for your self and for your art. After my homeless experience, any leftover pride was thankfully shattered.

At the same time I was going through the roughest financial time of my life, it was the most glorious time. I didn't blame God, although I wondered why He was allowing this to happen. Did He even have anything to do with the economy? God is sovereign over everything:

"Are not two sparrows sold for a penny? And not one of them will fall to the ground apart from your Father." Matthew 10:29

So if He is sovereign over everything, is He just watching the economy crash and me suffer with the rest of the world? Or should I count my blessings with my health and my children's health? Maybe I will focus on what is good instead of what is bad. Maybe we are to learn from these lessons and grow in our faith. Sleeping in my car and experiencing financial difficulty for a couple of years have humbled me and strengthened my faith-walk. I just pray that God keeps a roof over my head.

My homeless days ended, and I acquired a new respect for all those without a home to call their own. I pray daily for them and for the unemployed and those who are suffering through the economic downfall.

Despite losing everything, I basked in the kindness and providence of God, who used Dana to finally lead me to His path. The God who would make the man I previously misjudged, Rev. Frank Barker, a mentor and a father figure.

Your Journey

"And God is able to make all grace abound to you, so that having all sufficiency in all things at all times, you may abound in every good work."
2 Corinthians 9:8

_____

_____

_____

_____

_____

_____

_____

_____

_____

_____

_____

_____

_____

_____

The Unique Character of the Apostle Paul
by James Stalker

His character presented a wonderful combination of the natural and the spiritual. From nature he had received a strongly marked individuality; but the change which Christianity produces was no less obvious in him. In no saved man's character is it possible to separate nicely what is due to nature from what is due to grace; for nature and grace blend sweetly in the redeemed life. In Paul the union of the two was singularly complete; yet it was always clear that there were two elements in him of diverse origin; and this is, indeed, the key to a successful estimate of his character.

Physique.—To begin with what was most simply natural—his physique was an important condition of his career. As want of ear may make a musical career impossible or a failure of eyesight stop the progress of a painter, so the missionary life is impossible without a certain degree of physical stamina. To any one reading by itself the catalogue of Paul's sufferings and observing the elasticity with which he rallied from the severest of them and resumed his labors, it would naturally occur that he must have been a person of Herculean mold. On the contrary, he appears to have been little of stature, and his bodily presence was weak. This weakness seems to have been sometimes aggravated by disfiguring disease; and he felt keenly the disappointment which he knew his bodily presence would excite among strangers; for every preacher who loves his work would like to preach the gospel with all the graces which conciliate the favor of hearers to an orator. God, however, used his very weakness, beyond his hopes, to draw out the tenderness of his converts; and so, when he was weak, then he was strong, and he was able to glory even in his infirmities.

There is a theory, which has obtained extensive currency, that the disease he suffered from was violent ophthalmia, causing disagreeable redness of the eyelids. But its grounds are very slender. He seems, on the contrary, to have had a remarkable power of fascinating and cowing an enemy with the keenness of his glance, as in the story of Elymas the sorcerer, which reminds us of the tradition about Luther, that his eyes sometimes so glowed and sparkled that bystanders could scarcely look on them.

There is no foundation whatever for an idea of some recent biographers of Paul that his bodily constitution was excessively fragile and chronically afflicted with shattering nervous disease. No one could have gone through his labors or suffered the stoning, the scourgings and other tortures he endured without having an exceptionally tough and sound constitution. It is true that he was sometimes worn out with illness and torn down with the acts of violence to which he was exposed; but the rapidity of his recovery on such occasions proves what a large fund of bodily force he had to draw upon. And who can doubt that, when his face was melted with tender love in beseeching men to be reconciled to God or lighted up with enthusiasm in the delivery of his message, it must have possessed a noble beauty far above mere regularity of feature?

Enterprise.—There was a good deal that was natural in another element of his character on which much depended—his spirit of enterprise. There are many men who like to grow where they are born; to have to change into new circumstances and make acquaintance with new people is intolerable to them. But there are others who have a kind of vagabondism in the blood; they are the persons intended by nature for emigrants and pioneers; and, if they take to the work of the ministry, they make the best missionaries.

In modern times no missionary has had this consecrated spirit of adventure in the same degree as that great Scotchman, David Livingstone. When he first went to Africa, he found the missionaries clustered in the south of the continent, just within the fringe of heathenism; they had their houses and gardens, their families, their small congregations of natives; and they were content. But he moved at once away beyond the rest into the heart of heathenism, and dreams of more distant regions never ceased to haunt him, till at length he began his extraordinary tramps over thousands of miles where no missionary had ever been before; and, when death overtook him, he was still pressing forward.

Paul's was a nature of the same stamp, full of courage and adventure. The unknown in the distance, instead of dismaying, drew him on. He could not bear to build on other men's foundations, but was constantly hastening to virgin soil, leaving churches behind for others to build up. He believed that, if he lit the lamp of the gospel here and there over vast areas, the light would spread in his absence by its own virtue. He liked to count the leagues he had left behind him, but his watchword was ever Forward. In his dreams he saw men beckoning him to new countries; he had always a long unfulfilled program in his mind; and, as death approached, he was still thinking of journeys into the remotest corners of the known world.

Influence Over Men.—Another element of his character near akin to the one just mentioned was his influence over men. There are those to whom it is painful to have to accost a stranger even on pressing business; and most men are only quite at home in their own set—among men of the same class or profession as themselves. But the life he had chosen brought Paul into contact with men of every kind, and he had constantly to be introducing to strangers the business with which he was charged. He might be addressing a king or a consul the one hour and a roomful of slaves or common soldiers the next. One day he had to speak in the synagogue of the Jews, another among a crowd of Athenian philosophers, another to the inhabitants of some provincial town far from the seats of culture. But he could adapt himself to every man and every audience. To the Jews he spoke as a rabbi out of the Old Testament Scriptures; to the Greeks he quoted the words of their own poets; and to the barbarians he talked of the God who giveth rain from heaven and fruitful seasons, filling our hearts with food and gladness.

When a weak or insincere man attempts to be all things to all men, he ends by being nothing to anybody. But, living on this principle, Paul found entrance for the gospel everywhere, and at the same time won for himself the esteem and love of those to whom he stooped. If he was bitterly hated by enemies, there was never a man more intensely loved by his friends. They received him as an angel of God, or even as Jesus Christ himself, and were ready to pluck out their eyes and give them to him. One church was jealous of another getting too much of him. When he was not able to pay a visit at the time he had promised, they were furious, as if he had done them a wrong. When he was parting from them, they wept sore and fell on his neck and kissed him. Numbers of young men were continually about him, ready to go on his errands. It was the largeness of his manhood which was the secret of this fascination; for to a big nature all resort, feeling that in its neighborhood it is well with them.

Unselfishness.—This popularity was partly, however, due to another quality which shone conspicuously in his character—the spirit of unselfishness. This is the rarest quality in human nature, and it is the most powerful of all in its influence on others, where it exists in purity and strength. Most men are so absorbed in their own interests and so naturally expect others to be the same that, if they see any one who appears to have no interests of his own to serve but is willing to do as much for the sake of others as the generality do for themselves, they are at first incredulous, suspecting that he is only hiding his designs beneath the cloak of benevolence; but, if he stand the test and his unselfishness prove to be genuine, there is no limit to the homage they are prepared to pay him. As Paul appeared in country after country and city after city, he was at first a complete enigma to those whom he approached. They formed all sorts of conjectures as to his real design. Was it money he was seeking, or power, or something darker and less pure? His enemies never ceased to throw out such insinuations. But those who got near him and saw the man as he was, who knew that he refused money and worked with his hands day and night to keep himself above the suspicion of mercenary motives, who heard him pleading with them one by one in their homes and exhorting them with tears to a holy life, who saw the sustained personal interest he took in every one of them—these could not resist the proofs of his disinterestedness or deny him their affection.

There never was a man more unselfish; he had literally no interest of his own to live for. Without family ties, he poured all the affections of his big nature, which might have been given to wife and children, into the channels of his work. He compares his tenderness toward his converts to that of a nursing-mother to her children; he pleads with them to remember that he is their father who has begotten them in the gospel. They are his glory and crown, his hope and joy and crown of rejoicing. Eager as he was for new conquests, he never lost his hold upon those he had won. He could assure his churches that he prayed and gave thanks for them night and day, and he remembered his converts by name at the throne of grace. How could human nature resist disinterestedness like this? If Paul was a conqueror of the world, he conquered it by the power of love.

His Mission.—The two most distinctively Christian features of his character have still to be mentioned. One of these was the sense of having a divine mission to preach Christ, which he was bound to fulfill. Most men merely drift through life, and the work they do is determined by a hundred indifferent circumstances; they might as well be doing anything else, or they would prefer, if they could afford it, to be doing nothing at all. But, from the time when he became a Christian, Paul knew that he had a definite work to do; and the call he had received to it never ceased to ring like a tocsin in his soul. "Woe is unto me if I preach not the gospel;" this was the impulse which drove him on. He felt that he had a world of new truths to utter and that the salvation of mankind depended on their utterance. He knew himself called to make Christ known to as many of his fellow-creatures as his utmost exertions could enable him to reach. It was this which made him so impetuous in his movements, so blind to danger, so contemptuous of suffering. "None of these things move me, neither count I my life dear unto myself, so that I might finish my course with joy, and the ministry which I have received of the Lord Jesus, to testify the gospel of the grace of God." He lived with the account which he would have to give at the judgment-seat of Christ ever in his eye, and his heart was revived in every hour of discouragement by the vision of the crown of life which, if he proved faithful, the Lord; the righteous Judge, would place upon his head.

Devotion to Christ.—The other peculiarly Christian quality which shaped his career was personal devotion to Christ. This was the supreme characteristic of the man, and from first to last the mainspring of his activities. From the moment of his first meeting with Christ he had but one passion; his love to his Savior burned with more and more brightness to the end. He delighted to call himself the slave of Christ, and had no ambition except to be the propagator of His ideas and the continuer of His influence.

He took up this idea of being Christ's representative with startling boldness. He says the heart of Christ is beating in his bosom toward his converts; he says the mind of Christ is thinking in his brain; he says that he is continuing the work of Christ and filling up that which was lacking in His sufferings; he says the wounds of Christ are reproduced in the scars upon his body; he says he is dying that others may live, as Christ died for the life of the world. But it was in reality the deepest humility which lay beneath these bold expressions. He had the sense that Christ had done everything for him; He had entered into him, casting out the old Paul and ending the old life, and had begotten a new man, with new designs, feelings and activities. And it was his deepest longing that this process should go on and become complete—that his old self should vanish quite away, and that the new self, which Christ had created in His own image and still sustained, should become so predominant that, when the thoughts of his mind were Christ's thoughts, the words on his lips Christ's words, the deeds he did Christ's deeds, and the character he wore Christ's character, he might be able to say, "I live, yet not I, but Christ liveth in me."

CHAPTER EIGHT

My Mentor: Reverend Frank Barker

The Reverend Frank Barker

"So Barnabas went to Tarsus to look for Saul, and when he had found him, he brought him to Antioch. For a whole year they met with the church and taught a great many people. And in Antioch the disciples were first called Christians." Acts 11:25,26

The Salvation revelation with Dana in 2008 will forever mark the true beginning of my conversion from Islam to Christianity. My near-conversion in 1996, four years after surviving the aneurysm, would be the underbrush I had to clear to start the journey. One of those people who helped me with the underbrush of too many faiths was Rev. Frank Barker.

My initial meeting with Rev. Barker in 1996 was marked by my desire for a broad sweep of the brush, one that would allow everyone into Heaven. Frank embodies a heart of gold that takes on this entire world as a burden. He shared that burden with me at the time, as well as what I had to do to be *saved*. He told me that I had to believe in Christ to attain Salvation. That Salvation comes through Jesus and through His grace alone. Frank then read me this verse:

"The saying is trustworthy and deserving of full acceptance, that Christ Jesus came into the world to save sinners, of whom I am the foremost." 1 Timothy 1:15

I was intrigued by the verse and asked Frank who the writer was. He said the Apostle Paul wrote the verse. My knowledge of Paul was limited at the time. I hadn't read more than the *Road to Damascus* experience. I asked Frank why Paul wrote, ". . . of whom I am the foremost." Frank said that Paul considered himself to be chief of sinners. I couldn't understand how a man who wrote nearly half the books of the New Testament would be "chief of sinners." And why did Christ come to save sinners? Why are we sinners in the first place?

Frank traced back the subject of sin with me. He told me that since Adam and Eve fell from the garden, sin entered this world. First Cain killed Abel, then man continued to sin till our days. I was not convinced. I am a pretty good person, and Frank is much better than I. Why does he call himself a sinner? Upon asking again about the destiny of my family, Frank said, "Your family is in the hands of God; what are *you* going to do?" I walked out on Frank. I did not like being put on the spot. Our next meeting would be twelve long years later.

Frank's Story

Frank in the Navy

Frank grew up in a Christian home and thought of himself as a Christian: "I got the idea that if you believed that Christianity was true, and that Jesus was who He said He was, and if you were not too bad, then you were a Christian. I didn't understand that faith was not just believing, but trusting in Him for my Salvation. I had not surrendered my will to him but lived my life my way. My God was peer pressure, being part of the group, and doing what the crowd wanted."

Frank became a fighter pilot in the Navy. While on aircraft carriers, he had many close calls that led him closer to God. Catapulting his plane, the Cougar, off the carrier was the toughest task. In fact, many died trying to do just that. These are a few of the ten things he had to remember as his plane blasted off: "Lean my head back so not to snap my neck. Pull my elbow into my stomach so I don't pull the stick back, stalling the plane and spinning into the water. Take my feet off the breaks so not to blow both tires up. Adjust the wings."

The first time he was about to take off, he couldn't remember the tenth requirement. The Catapult Officer kept waving and waiting for Frank to salute, the sign for them to launch the plane. Frank finally saluted, and the plane shot off. Within a second, the tenth requisite was as clear as the g-force pulling on his body. The Catapult Grip, a little metal bar, had to be gripped with the throttle, or the throttle would back off and the jet would end up in the water with the carrier running over it. As the jet was falling into the sea, he jammed the throttle forward at the last second, and the plane skimmed the water and made it up. Frank breathed a huge sigh of relief.

While in training, he hung out with his buddies drinking and partying and never considered religion. He was living the life of a Navy fighter pilot who didn't have time for anything but the good times. Frank's training took place in Pensacola, Florida. One weekend while driving back from Birmingham, he fell asleep at the wheel. The road curved to the right and his car went straight along a dirt road. He woke up scared and slammed on the breaks. The car slid to a screeching halt. As the dust settled, the lights of his car were shining on a sign that read, "The wages of sin is death."

Frank was stunned. "I felt God was trying to tell me something." He went back to his Navy training with a different attitude and made some changes. He tried to be good, but the temptations were too strong. Then he decided to go to seminary: "I had to go to seminary to become a good Christian." He attended Colombia Theological Seminary in Decatur, Georgia. At the same time, he became a part-time pastor at Dobson Memorial Presbyterian Church in Oxford, Alabama.

Frank's Conversion

After a year of seminary training he realized something was missing. He wondered, "How can I know for sure that I am Christian?" There was an Air Force chaplain at the seminary that he felt free to talk to and asked him, "What does it mean to believe in Jesus?" The chaplain gave him a track that explained it: "It does not mean just to believe that Jesus is true, but to also trust in Jesus as your approach to God." Frank's reaction was, "That is too easy, that would be a gift. God isn't going to give us Salvation, we have to earn it by our good deeds."

He was reading the Bible to prove the track wrong, and suddenly hit Romans 6:23: *"The wages of sin is death."* The verse he had seen on that sign when his car veered off the road! But he had never seen the rest of the verse: *"but the free gift of God is eternal life in Christ Jesus our Lord."* His reaction was, "Good night!! *It is a gift!"* He realized that Salvation was by grace, and while he had believed in Christ, he had not trusted in Him, but had thought in terms of earning Salvation. That was when Frank placed his trust in Jesus and became a Christian.

Machen and Warfield

While at Oxford, he was cleaning a closet where he stayed and found a book by J. Gresham Machen, *Christianity and Liberalism.* "After reading it, I said to myself, 'That is what I am in the middle of: my seminary was heading in a liberal direction.'" Frank would later become instrumental in forming the conservative PCA (Presbyterian Church of America) denomination. The PCA is the third largest Presbyterian Church body and the largest conservative Reformed denomination in the United States.

While at seminary, one of Frank's courses was to read a Christian writer and learn everything about him. "I wanted to read Machen. The teacher said that Machen was not a Southern Presbyterian, but his mother was! So they let me read Machen. Then I was introduced to B.B. Warfield, and I read everything Warfield wrote. That is where I got my theology," Frank says.

Note: It may be appropriate here to mention that the publisher of this book, Mike Gaydosh, chose B. B. Warfield, J. Gresham Machen, and James Stalker to provide the Pauline commentary before he met Rev. Frank Barker. While being extremely familiar with Warfield and Machen, Frank was not as astute with Stalker's work. I have since shared with Frank this story: When Warfield was working on an article, "The Religious Life of the Seminary Student," he wrote to James Stalker and asked for the five most influential books of his spiritual life. This shows how much Warfield valued Stalker's opinion. The fact that these giants were chosen by Mike while being a foundational source for Frank makes writing this book along side these masterful and gifted minds very humbling. Another confirmation is the book by Adolph Monod that was one of Stalker's essentials, Saint Paul.

Frank's faith would strengthen while he was pastoring Dobson Memorial. He would finish seminary and move back to Birmingham to establish Briarwood Presbyterian Church in 1960, which would grow to several thousand members. Through the church, Frank has formed ministries such as Campus Outreach, Birmingham Theological Seminary, and Young Business Leaders; as well as planted numerous churches around the world. In 2006, *The Church Report* listed Briarwood as the thirty-fifth most influential non-Catholic church in America.

Reconnecting Twelve Years Later

Frank and me

The year was 2008. It was after my Salvation conversation with Dana, and I was living a different life. I thought about Frank's words from that day in 1996 almost daily: "Your family is in the hands of God; what are you going to do?" I continued my work as a photographer. One evening, I was to photograph a dinner at the political think tank, The Alabama Policy Institute. I started shooting the speakers, then sat down for the dinner break with a few people who were courteous and friendly. They quickly asked where I was from, and I shared with them an abbreviated version of my testimony. Upon learning they attended Briarwood, I said, "I would love to see Rev. Frank Barker. I have something to tell him."

The woman next to me smiled and said, "If you turn around, you can probably touch him. He is sitting right behind you."

I turned around and saw Frank and his wife Barbara. I got up and knelt by his chair and said, "Hello Dr. Barker, do you remember me?"

"No," said Frank, who is a man of a few words.

I said, "Twelve years ago, you told me that Jesus Christ was the only way to Heaven. I grew up a Muslim and had struggled with that idea."

"And?" he said firmly.

"Now I consider Him my Lord and Savior, and I am in peace with His Salvation," I said.

Barbara was listening. She smiled and mouthed the words "Praise God." Frank said, "Good." Then he added, "Can you have lunch with me tomorrow?"

The next day I met Frank for lunch, and since the fall of 2008, we have met weekly for a Bible study. I am always reminded of how blessed I am that he devotes time for me, although that is his strength: mentoring and leading others. I still know how occupied he is. He does not use an electronic calendar but still writes in a small notebook. When we finish a session and plan when to meet next, he pulls the calendar out of his pocket and opens it to extremely full pages. He always manages to fit me into his busy schedule.

I am genuinely thankful for Frank. He has become much more than a mentor. He has become a father figure that I see several times a week. He and Barbara have opened their home to me, and I stayed there for four months during my homeless days. I attend a Bible study at his house every Thursday night, and occasionally I come to the Prayer Breakfast they hold on Saturday. Frank and Barbara do nothing but *live* the Word.

Two Men I Love

Frank reminds me of my father, who was exact in all of his dealings, old school, and lovingly blunt. He said what was on his mind and only used words to achieve a goal. There was no chit-chat with my father, all while having a heart so big it took on the whole world. Dad worried about children everywhere and would voice these worries occasionally. At the same time, he loved life and cherished the small things. My father had a collection of utterances that resembled sayings of Frank's. They are also jolly joke tellers. A few of Frank's favorite's follow:

The little boy was asked to define a lie. He said, "A lie is an abomination to the Lord, and a very present help in time of trouble."

A little boy said, "When I die, I want to die like my granddaddy: quiet and in my sleep. Not screaming and hollering like the people in the car with him."

When Frank tells a joke, he laughs more than the people listening do - and so did my father. Another one of Frank's favorites:

Three people were viewing the dead body of a friend in the casket. One of them said, "When it is our turn, what would you want people to say when they look at you?"

The first one said, "I would want them to say: 'He was a good man.'" The second one said, "I would want them to say, 'He was a faithful man.'" The third one said, "Not me, I would want them to say, 'LOOK, he is moving!'"

My father was from a small town in Syria called Homs. If you were from Homs, you were the victim of many jokes. Homsi people were smart and sweet, but the jokes portrayed them as lacking in intelligence. Dad had a few favorites:

Q: How do you keep a Homsi busy all day?
A: Put him in a round room and tell him to sit in the corner.

Q: How do you make a Homsi laugh on Saturday?
A: Tell him a joke on Wednesday.

Q: How did the Homsi try to kill the bird?
A: He threw it from a cliff.

Dad loved to make fun of himself, a sign of security and humility. Frank does also. On a serious note, the biggest thing they have in common is my love for them. Both men had a sincere interest in seeing me do my best.

The Apostle Paul

To Frank, Paul's conversion was one of the most paramount and significant events in Christian history: "Paul was against Christians and did everything in his power to oppress them. He was the number one persecutor who would become the number one promoter. What a tremendous argument for the resurrection: For him to become an instrument spreading Christianity among the Gentiles and becoming their Apostle. He would plant countless key churches all over Europe and Asia Minor. His letters are a key part of the foundation of Christianity."

Recently Frank and I studied the conversion of Saint Paul. He said that many people have conversion stories, but Paul's is different because of the results. God chose Paul before the foundation of the world to become His servant. He told him, "You will suffer many things for my name." And he did. He was imprisoned for years, and then finally martyred. Paul's conversion according to Frank was one of the defining moments in human history, not just Christianity.

Frank considers Paul's letter to the Romans as the most doctrinal and exegetical book in the Bible: "He gives the Romans the core truth. The book covers the entire doctrine of the Christian faith. After starting Briarwood, new members had to study four books; one of them was the book of Romans. It is an essential book to growing in faith."

I have studied some of Frank's favorite Pauline verses with him, and they have had a huge effect on my walk with the Lord. Below are a few:

Romans 3:24-26: *" . . . . and are justified by his grace as a gift, through the redemption that is in Christ Jesus, whom God put forward as a propitiation by his blood, to be received by faith. This was to show God's righteousness, because in his divine forbearance he had passed over former sins. It was to show his righteousness at the present time, so that he might be just and the justifier of the one who has faith in Jesus."*

Romans 8:1,2: *"There is therefore now no condemnation for those who are in Christ Jesus. For the law of the Spirit of life has set you free in Christ Jesus from the law of sin and death."*

Romans 8:28: *"And we know that for those who love God all things work together for good, for those who are called according to his purpose."*

Romans 12:1: *"I appeal to you therefore, brothers, by the mercies of God, to present your bodies as a living sacrifice, holy and acceptable to God, which is your spiritual worship."*

1 Corinthians 13: *"If I speak in the tongues of men and of angels, but have not love, I am a noisy gong or a clanging cymbal. And if I have prophetic powers, and understand all mysteries and all knowledge, and if I have all faith, so as to remove mountains, but have not love, I am nothing. If I give away all I have, and if I deliver up my body to be burned, but have not love, I gain nothing. Love is patient and kind; love does not envy or boast; it is not arrogant or rude. It does not insist on its own way; it is not irritable or resentful; it does not rejoice at wrongdoing, but rejoices with the truth. Love bears all things, believes all things, hopes all things, endures all things. Love never ends. As for prophecies, they will pass away; as for tongues, they will cease; as for knowledge, it will pass away. For we know in part and we prophesy in part, but when the perfect comes, the partial will pass away. When I was a child, I spoke like a child, I thought like a child, I reasoned like a child. When I became a man, I gave up childish ways. For now we see in a mirror dimly, but then face to face. Now I know in part; then I shall know fully, even as I have been fully known. So now faith, hope, and love abide, these three; but the greatest of these is love."*

2 Corinthians 4:16-5:8: *"So we do not lose heart. Though our outer self is wasting away, our inner self is being renewed day by day. For this light momentary affliction is preparing for us an eternal weight of glory beyond all comparison, as we look not to the things that are seen but to the things that are unseen. For the things that are seen are transient, but the things that are unseen are eternal. For we know that if the tent that is our earthly* *home is destroyed, we have a building from God, a house not made with hands, eternal in the heavens. For in this tent we groan, longing to put on our heavenly dwelling, if indeed by putting it on we may not be found naked. For while we are still in this tent, we groan, being burdened—not that we would be unclothed, but that we would be further clothed, so that what is mortal may be swallowed up by life. He who has prepared us for this very thing is God, who has given us the Spirit as a guarantee. So we are always of good courage. We know that while we are at home in the body we are away from the Lord, for we walk by faith, not by sight. Yes, we are of good courage, and we would rather be away from the body and at home with the Lord."*

2 Corinthians 10:4,5: *"For the weapons of our warfare are not of the flesh but have divine power to destroy strongholds. We destroy arguments and every lofty opinion raised against the knowledge of God, and take every thought captive to obey Christ,"*

Galatians 2:20: *"I have been crucified with Christ. It is no longer I who live, but Christ who lives in me. And the life I now live in the flesh I live by faith in the Son of God, who loved me and gave himself for me."*

Galatians 5:22-25: *"But the fruit of the Spirit is love, joy, peace, patience, kindness, goodness, faithfulness, gentleness, self-control; against such things there is no law. And those who belong to Christ Jesus have crucified the flesh with its passions and desires. If we live by the Spirit, let us also walk by the Spirit."*

Ephesians 2:8,9: *"For by grace you have been saved through faith. And this is not your own doing; it is the gift of God, not a result of works, so that no one may boast."*

Philippians 1:21: *"For to me, to live is Christ and to die is gain."*

Philippians 4:13: *"I can do all things through him who strengthens me."*

1 Thessalonians 4:16-18: *"For the Lord himself will descend from heaven with a cry of command, with the voice of an archangel, and with the sound of the trumpet of God. And the dead in Christ will rise first. Then we who are alive, who are left, will be caught up together with them in the clouds to meet the Lord in the air, and so we will always be with the Lord. Therefore encourage one another with these words."*

2 Timothy 4:1,2: *"I charge you in the presence of God and of Christ Jesus, who is to judge the living and the dead, and by his appearing and his kingdom: preach the word; be ready in season and out of season; reprove, rebuke, and exhort, with complete patience and teaching."*

And the last one is the dearest to Frank. It is when Paul had a thorn in his flesh:

2 Corinthians 12:9,10: *"But he said to me, 'My grace is sufficient for you, for my power is made perfect in weakness.' Therefore I will boast all the more gladly of my weaknesses, so that the power of Christ may rest upon me. For the sake of Christ, then, I am content with weaknesses, insults, hardships, persecutions, and calamities. For when I am weak, then I am strong."*

Pastor Harry Reeder

Frank Barker started Briarwood Presbyterian Church in 1960 and was the senior pastor till the fall of 1999. Upon retirement, Frank and a search committee chose Harry Reeder to be the senior pastor at Briarwood. Harry had planted a PCA church in Charlotte, North Carolina, seventeen years before his coming to Briarwood.

In February of 1983, Pastor Reeder was called to Christ Covenant Presbyterian Church as their founding pastor. The ministry began with thirty-eight committed members and in seventeen years, attendance grew to over three thousand people. Harry also leads a growing Bible teaching radio ministry called *In Perspective*. The program is heard Monday through Friday on a number of stations in the southeast.

He is devoted to the ministry of church revitalization, hosting multiple "Embers to a Flame Conferences" both nationally and internationally each year. Pastor Reeder completed his doctoral dissertation on The Biblical Paradigm of Church Revitalization; received his Doctor of Ministry Degree from Reformed Theological Seminary, Charlotte, North Carolina (where he serves as adjunct faculty member and holds the same status at Birmingham Theological Seminary, Birmingham, Alabama); and is the author

of *From Embers to a Flame – How God Can Revitalize Your Church.*
Pastor Harry Reeder is married to Cindy, and they have three children.

He says this of Frank: "Frank Barker has been a model and a
mentor for me as a Christian man and as a Pastor for almost the
entire span of my life in ministry. Now, to enjoy the privilege of
continuing that relationship in the context of a collegial relationship at Briarwood where he serves as Pastor Emeritus is only an
added blessing. Frank exemplifies an unstoppable commitment
to fulfill the Great Commission by 'making disciples of all the nations' through our Lord's church, the Body and Bride of Christ.
His walk in the Lord and for the Lord demonstrates a quiet security in the saving grace of Christ while manifesting the transforming grace of Christ by his unabashed love for Him. Frank's
relentless commitment to learn of Christ from His Word and his
submission through the practice of persistent intercessory prayer
continually exalts Christ and multiplies his faithful effectiveness
in serving the Lord."

Frank and Barbara

Frank and Barbara Barker

To count all that Frank and Barbara have done for the community of Birmingham and the entire world would fill pages. Barbara helps Frank with all the Bible studies and prayer meetings they lead at their home. She also teaches ballet at the church. She has also written the book *Faith Pointes, Essential Truths for Living the Christian Life*. They are involved in many ministries and support countless missionaries all over the world.

Barbara teaches seven Bible studies per week. "I had two more that I stopped," she says smiling. She considers being married to Frank the biggest blessing: "You have never seen such submission to the Lord. He does not do anything for himself. He has this little notebook with prayers all over it, and he will sit there for hours praying." They often pray together. Barbara thinks of Frank as much more than an earthly partner: "We have the same heart, the same goals. We pray for our children and grandchildren, the church, the community, and whatever the Lord puts on our hearts."

Frank continues to sharpen my sword. The knowledge I gain from him has enabled me to take on the role of a mentor with a recent friend who asked me to meet with him every week so we can grow in faith together. Two weeks prior, my friend woke up feeling like he had to know more about Christ. I was thrilled at his request. It was what Saint Paul did with Timothy and Titus after having Barnabas as his mentor.

In addition to adopting Frank as a teacher and a father, my life in this country continues to be full of twists and turns, one of which would come into full view regarding my American citizenship. The freedom we live here is precious beyond measure, and yet, that same freedom is capable of leading to what is utterly despicable. I would get an assignment that would entwine the evil of hate with the beauty of freedom. This photo shoot would reveal liberty as real as the hoods they were wearing.

Your Journey

"Therefore, my beloved brothers, be steadfast, immovable, always abounding in the work of the Lord, knowing that in the Lord your labor is not in vain." 1 Corinthians 15:58

_____

_____

_____

_____

_____

_____

_____

_____

_____

_____

_____

_____

_____

_____

Paul's Imprisonment and Appeal to Caesar
by James Stalker

Paul's Return to Jerusalem.—After completing his brief visit to Greece at the close of his third missionary journey, Paul returned to Jerusalem. He must by this time have been nearly sixty years of age; and for twenty years he had been engaged in almost superhuman labors. He had been traveling and preaching incessantly, and carrying on his heart a crushing weight of cares. His body had been worn with disease and mangled with punishments and abuse; and his hair must have been whitened, and his face furrowed with the lines of age. As yet, however, there were no signs of his body breaking down, and his spirit was still as keen as ever in its enthusiasm for the service of Christ.

His eye was specially directed to Rome, and, before leaving Greece, he sent word to the Romans that they might expect to see him soon. But, as he was hurrying toward Jerusalem along the shores of Greece and Asia, the signal sounded that his work was nearly done, and the shadow of approaching death fell across his path. In city after city the persons in the Christian communities who were endowed with the gift of prophecy foretold that bonds and imprisonment were awaiting him, and, as he came nearer to the close of his journey, these warnings became more loud and frequent. He felt their solemnity; his was a brave heart, but it was too humble and reverent not to be overawed with the thought of death and judgment. He had several companions with him, but he sought opportunities of being alone. He parted from his converts as a dying man, telling them that they would see his face no more. But, when they entreated him to turn back and avoid the threatened danger, he gently pushed aside their loving arms, and said, "What mean ye to weep and to break my heart? for I am ready not to be bound only, but also to die at Jerusalem for the name of the Lord Jesus."

We do not know what business he had on hand which so peremptorily demanded his presence in Jerusalem. He had to deliver up to the apostles a collection on behalf of their poor saints, which he had been exerting himself to gather in the Gentile churches; and it may have been of importance that he should discharge this service in person. Or he may have been solicitous to procure from the apostles a message for his Gentile churches, giving an authoritative contradiction to the insinuations of his enemies as to the un-apostolic character of his gospel. At all events there was some imperative call of duty summoning him, and, in spite of the fear of death and the tears of friends, he went forward to his fate.

Paul's Arrest.—It was the feast of Pentecost when he arrived in the city of his fathers, and, as usual at such seasons, Jerusalem was crowded with hundreds of thousands of pilgrim Jews from all parts of the world. Among these there could not but be many who had seen him at the work of evangelization in the cities of the heathen and come into collision with him there. Their rage against him had been checked in foreign lands by the interposition of Gentile authority; but might they not, if they met with him in the Jewish capital, wreak on him their vengeance with the support of the whole population?

This was actually the danger into which he fell. Certain Jews from Ephesus, the principal scene of his labors during his third journey, recognized him in the temple and, crying out that here was the heretic who blasphemed the Jewish nation, law and temple, brought about him in an instant a raging sea of fanaticism. It is a wonder he was not torn limb from limb on the spot; but superstition prevented his assailants from defiling with blood the court of the Jews, in which he was caught, and, before they got him hustled into the court of the Gentiles, where they would soon have dispatched him, the Roman guard, whose sentries were pacing the castle-ramparts which overlooked the temple-courts, rushed down and took him under their protection; and, when their captain learned that he was a Roman citizen, his safety was secured.

But the fanaticism of Jerusalem was now thoroughly aroused, and it raged against the protection which surrounded Paul like an angry sea. The Roman captain on the day after the apprehension took him down to the Sanhedrin in order to ascertain the charge against him; but the sight of the prisoner created such an uproar that he had to hurry him away, lest he should be torn in pieces. Strange city and strange people! There was never a nation which produced sons more richly dowered with gifts to make her name immortal; there was never a city whose children clung to her with a more passionate affection; yet, like a mad mother, she tore the very goodliest of them in pieces and dashed them mangled from her breast. Jerusalem was now within a few years of her destruction; here was the last of her inspired and prophetic sons come to visit her for the last time, with boundless love to her in his heart; but she would have murdered him; and only the shields of the Gentiles saved him from her fury.

Forty zealots banded themselves together under a curse to snatch Paul even from the midst of the Roman swords; and the Roman captain was only able to foil their plot by sending him under a heavy escort down to Caesarea. This was a Roman city on the Mediterranean coast; it was the residence of the Roman governor of Palestine and the headquarters of the Roman garrison; and in it the apostle was perfectly safe from Jewish violence.

His Imprisonment at Caesarea.—Here he remained in prison for two years. The Jewish authorities attempted again and again either to procure his condemnation by the governor or to get him delivered up to themselves, to be tried as an ecclesiastical offender; but they failed to convince the governor that Paul had been guilty of any crime of which he could take cognizance or to persuade him to hand over a Roman citizen to their tender mercies. The prisoner ought to have been released, but his enemies were so vehement in asserting that he was a criminal of the deepest dye that he was detained on the chance of new evidence turning up against him. Besides, his release was prevented by the expectation of the corrupt governor, Felix, that the life of the leader of a religious sect might be purchased from him with a bribe. Felix was interested in his prisoner and even heard him gladly, as Herod had listened to the Baptist.

Paul was not kept in close confinement; he had at least the range of the barracks in which he was detained. There we can imagine him pacing the ramparts on the edge of the Mediterranean, and gazing wistfully across the blue waters in the direction of Macedonia, Achaia and Ephesus, where his spiritual children were pining for him or perhaps encountering dangers in which they sorely needed his presence.

It was a mysterious providence which thus arrested his energies and condemned the ardent worker to inactivity. Yet we can see now the reason for it. Paul was needing rest. After twenty years of incessant evangelization he required leisure to garner the harvest of experience. During all that time he had been preaching that view of the gospel which at the beginning of his Christian career he had thought out, under the influence of the revealing Spirit, in the solitudes of Arabia. But he had now reached a stage when, with leisure to think, he might penetrate into more recondite regions of the truth as it is in Jesus. And it was so important that he should have this leisure that, in order to secure it, God even permitted him to be shut up in prison.

Paul's Later Gospel.—During these two years he wrote nothing; it was a time of internal mental activity and silent progress. But, when he began to write again, the results of it were at once discernible. The Epistles written after this imprisonment have a mellower tone and set forth a profounder view of doctrine than his earlier writings. There is no contradiction, indeed, or inconsistency between his earlier and later views: in Ephesians and Colossians he builds on the broad foundations laid in Romans and Galatians. But the superstructure is loftier and more imposing. He dwells less on the work of Christ and more on His person; less on the justification of the sinner and more on the sanctification of the saint.

In the gospel revealed to him in Arabia he had set Christ forth as dominating mundane history, and shown His first coming to be the point toward which the destinies of Jews and Gentiles had been tending. In the gospel revealed to him at Caesarea the point of view is extra-mundane: Christ is represented as the reason for the creation of all things, and as the Lord of angels and of worlds, to whose second coming the vast procession of the universe is moving forward—of whom, and through whom, and to whom are all things.

In the earlier Epistles the initial act of the Christian life—the justification of the soul—is explained with exhaustive elaboration: but in the later Epistles it is on the subsequent relations to Christ of the person who has been already justified that the apostle chiefly dwells. According to his teaching, the whole spectacle of the Christian life is due to a union between Christ and the soul; and for the description of this relationship he has invented a vocabulary of phrases and illustrations: believers are in Christ, and Christ is in them: they have the same relation to Him as the stones of a building to the foundation-stone, as the branches to the tree, as the members to the head, as a wife to her husband. This union is ideal, for the divine mind in eternity made the destiny of Christ and the believer one; it is legal, for their debts and merits are common property; it is vital, for the connection with Christ supplies the power of a holy and progressive life; it is moral, for, in mind and heart, in character and conduct, Christians are constantly becoming more and more identical with Christ.

His Ethics.—Another feature of these later Epistles is the balance between their theological and their moral teaching. This is visible even in the external structure of the greatest of them, for they are nearly equally divided into two parts, the first of which is occupied with doctrinal statements and the second with moral exhortations. The ethical teaching of Paul spreads itself over all parts of the Christian life; but it is not distinguished by a systematic arrangement of the various kinds of duties, although the domestic duties are pretty fully treated. Its chief characteristic lies in the motives which it brings to bear upon conduct.

To Paul Christian morality was emphatically a morality of motives. The whole history of Christ, not in the details of His earthly life, but in the great features of his redemptive journey from heaven to earth and from earth back to heaven again, as seen from the extramundane standpoint of these Epistles, is a series of examples to be copied by Christians in their daily conduct. No duty is too small to illustrate one or other of the principles which inspired the divinest acts of Christ. The commonest acts of humility and beneficence are to be imitations of the condescension which brought Him from the position of equality with God to the obedience of the cross; and the ruling motive of the love and kindness practiced by Christians to one another is to be the recollection of their common connection with Him.

Appeal to Caesar.—After Paul's imprisonment had lasted for two years, Felix was succeeded in the governorship of Palestine by Festus. The Jews had never ceased to intrigue to get Paul into their hands, and they at once assailed the new ruler with further importunities. As Festus seemed to be wavering, Paul availed himself of his privilege of appeal as a Roman citizen and demanded to be sent to Rome and tried at the bar of the emperor. This could not be refused him; and a prisoner had to be sent to Rome at once after such an appeal was taken. Very soon, therefore, Paul was shipped off under the charge of Roman soldiers and in the company of many other prisoners on their way to the same destination.

CHAPTER NINE

My Dual Citizenship in America and in Christ

"It is for freedom that Christ has set us free. Stand firm, then, and do not let yourselves be burdened again by a yoke of slavery." Galatians 5:1

My father always said, "They have too much freedom (Hurria) in the United States." I think you either have it or you don't. There can never be "too much" freedom. Freedom brings with it all kinds of stories, but it is much better to live under its shade than in the blaze of oppression. Growing up in Syria's *limited freedom* has taught me to appreciate what we have in this country.

Freedom in Syria is tainted by corruption. The recent Arab Spring is a testament to that fact, as young people in the Arab world are fed up with the status quo and absence of the democratic voice. It started in Tunisia and moved to Egypt, Libya, Syria, Bahrain, Yemen, and other countries. Syria has been in civil war for over two years, and many have died. I pray for peace to reign as the Arab world tries to come to terms with democracy. Syria has seen many conflicts and invasions from Romans to Mongols to Crusaders to Turks. Recently the government has used tanks, gunfire, and mass arrests to crush the revolution that started in 2011.

We have no idea what we take for granted in the Untied States. As a photojournalist for twenty-five years, I have experienced up close and personal this freedom I now cherish. In 2000, a story I will never forget took place: I was asked to photograph a Ku Klux Klan rally on the steps of the Jefferson County Courthouse. Really? I thought the KKK was a relic of the 60s, when they marched and set crosses on fire. They hated the blacks, the Jews, and anyone else who was not cut from the same bigoted mold. And now despite the birth of a new century, they were protesting on the steps of the courthouse in the middle of downtown Birmingham in broad daylight - reality check anyone?

The KKK protested on the steps of the
Jefferson County Courthouse in the year 2000.

The police protecting the KKK included many African-Americans.

I drove downtown and parked the car a few blocks away as the roads leading to the courthouse were blocked. I turned the corner and saw a scene that sent shivers up my spine. There they were with their hooded white robes yelling obscenities and spewing hatred and rage. At first I was repulsed by their display. How can they be allowed to do this on the steps of the courthouse? It has to be a mistake. This may be too much freedom, like my father used to say.

After calming down a bit, I saw something more shocking than the KKK. The police had erected a fence around the protesters *to protect them*. I had to take a second look. Both black and white policemen stood at attention keeping the angry mob of people away from the KKK and their hate-filled white hoods. I never saw freedom so sweet, and I never sensed such a filthy affair wrapped with a beautiful covering of duty and reverence. What I was witnessing was a true testament to freedom and how expensive it is. It brought tears to my eyes.

Here was the KKK, a group that uses this precious freedom to further their disgusting goals. And there were the police, facing the crowds and protecting the KKK, the same people who hate them. I looked closely at the face of a black police officer and wondered what he was thinking. I could hear the police chief prepping his officers for the event: "Men, it does not matter what these people stand for, and whether you agree with it or not. What matters is that they have obtained a permit, and they have the right to speak their minds. We have to protect them." If I were one of the police officers, I would have argued with him and might have done something stupid. This officer and all of the others were doing their admirable and honorable job of protecting free speech. Back in my former world, they would have certainly clobbered the KKK members and hauled them off to jail at the very least.

This event is ingrained in my brain because of the beauty of a justice system that says all are equal and every voice will be heard. I took some photographs that will always remind me how sweet freedom is.

My American Citizenship

This young Korean girl was getting her
citizenship the same day I got mine.

I became an American citizen in 1988, four years after I came to this country. It was one of the happiest days of my life. I had to study American history and government and take an exam. I passed and the ceremony was held at the courthouse in Knoxville, Tennessee. I lined up with about sixty people from different countries. The judge articulated what this country offers its citizens and all of the benefits of becoming an American citizen. He spoke of a free society where everyone is equal, where a person can accomplish anything within the law. Then he declared us all citizens of the United States of America. There were hugs and tears and much joy.

It wouldn't hit me until a week later. I had just become a citizen of a country so precious that multitudes have risked death to live here. My awareness of this privilege has never waned. I am always astounded at the fact that we can elect our officials, and that we can vote for the president - and our votes count. We can voice our opinions for or against the government. I hear people complaining about the political corruption, and I can't help but think: American corruption would be an appetizer on the menu in other parts of the world where tyranny, extortion, and bribery are the main courses.

I have thrived as a photographer and a writer in a country where free speech shines. There are no limits to what you can do. Commentators will flat out criticize what the government is doing in newspapers and on television. That is such a foreign concept for me. The government does not control the media? I have had the privilege of photographing many presidents and famous people over the years, and knowing them has marked my citizenship with reverence and adoration for what this country stands for.

Photojournalism

Working as a photojournalist has been a series of adventures, and my camera has given me access to many amazing people, including some of America's most beloved celebrities: Bill Cosby, Loretta Lynn, Morgan Freeman, Norah Jones, Hank Williams III, Mick Jagger, Stevie Wonder, Taylor Hicks, Jerry Garcia, and Michael Jordan, just to name a few.

I photographed the dedication of the Selma-to-Montgomery March at the Edmund Pettus Bridge in Selma, Alabama.

I also have photographed major events like the commemoration of the Civil Rights March on the Edmund Pettus Bridge in Selma. The march, also known as Bloody Sunday, was held in 1965 and marked the political and emotional peak of the American civil rights movement. It was incredible to feel what the marchers felt on the bridge as they were attacked by dogs and fire hoses.

Shooting major events and famous people has been a pleasure I cherish. One of my most memorable episodes was with legendary country music singer/songwriter Loretta Lynn.

Loretta Lynn (I photographed Loretta for Southern Living magazine)

Loretta Lynn sang me "Coal Miner's Daughter" at her house in Waverly, Tennessee.

Arriving at her mansion in Middle Tennessee on a hot summer day, I drove up the driveway surrounded by massive trees. Her assistant ushered me into a huge parlor filled with elaborate furniture. He announced needing to take care of something outside while motioning me to a chair.

Without warning, Loretta Lynn hobbled in with one boot on, and the other stuck halfway down in an uncomfortable position. She was dressed in tight jeans and a colorful shirt; the years have been gentle with her beauty. She looked astounding to be a woman of her age.

She looked around and asked where her assistant was. I replied that he stepped out for a minute. Shrugging, she asked me to help her with her boot. I made my way to the doorway where she stood and knelt in front of her. I pulled the boot on from the back as she squeezed her foot in. She held on to my head to keep her balance, and I couldn't help but laugh and wonder why there was no video camera around!

She playfully rumpled my hair and said that she liked the curls, as I blushed and laughed. Finally, she asked me who I was, and I explained that I was the photographer with Southern Living magazine. Her eyes grew big and she quickly apologized and pulled me up, placing her arm around me and leading me back into a room filled with makeup people and more assistants.

I began taking pictures and she asked me if I had ever heard her song "Coal Miner's Daughter." I felt a little embarrassed as I had not developed a taste for country music, so I was unfamiliar with the song. I told her that it had been a long time. She asked me to sit on her bed. Then she sat next to me and sang with her gorgeous voice as the makeup crew and assistants all stood in awe. We took more pictures then went into the parlor for the formal portrait. She kept teasing me about the boot, and she was as lovely as can be. She smiled mischievously and said she was going to write a song named *Karim* . . . Of course, I am still waiting.

I left that day while pondering the unique access this job has afforded me to become close to these social icons for a magical couple of hours. I also reflected on the opportunity this country provides its people. Here is a poor coal miner's daughter who would grow up to be one of the most beloved singers of all time. Only in America, only in this country you can accomplish any goal no matter how unattainable it may seem.

Another memorable event was photographing Morgan Freeman for *People* magazine. I arrived at his birthplace, Clarksdale, Mississippi, where he honorably chose to live despite the prevalent poverty. It was a typical Delta town with its boarded-up downtown buildings and austere surroundings, except for his blues club, *Ground Zero*. The club was spacious and beautifully decorated with the appeal of antiquity.

*Morgan Freeman and I spent time together a couple of years ago
at his blues club, Ground Zero, in Cleveland, Mississippi.*

Morgan Freeman (photographed here for People magazine)

Morgan was a genuine man with humility and humor. The
night was a special one, as they were celebrating the one-year
anniversary of his club. During the shoot, I directed him with
ease, asking him to look this way and that. He obliged and did
everything with the comfort and grace of someone who relished
the camera.

At one point, I asked him to look at Amy, my assistant who
was standing in the corner of the room. He started winking and
making faces while pointing at her with his hand in a gun pose. I
laughed as I was shooting. When we were finished, he asked us to
stay for the party. There was dancing, singing, and people having
a good time. I was shooting him dancing with his wife when she

decided her feet had seen enough action, so she sat down. Instead of following her, Morgan turned and motioned for me to come closer and join the fans dancing with him. So I did.

Would anyone believe this? I was dancing with Morgan Freeman! Once more, all I could think was that here I was, a photographer who could not photograph this once-in-a-lifetime moment. We danced less than a minute until his fans took over the scene. I pulled back and began shooting again. I kept thinking throughout the night how refreshing it was to see a giant like Morgan Freeman acting like he was a regular at the club.

The evening ended and we said good-bye and headed back to Birmingham. I was struck with how genuine Morgan was. I have always enjoyed photographing people who are larger than life. Celebrities are an interesting subculture, and not at all what most people think they are. Some of them can be kind and sincere.

Whether I am photographing a Selma march, a KKK rally, Loretta Lynn, or Morgan Freeman, I can always be sure that we live in a free country where our right to vote is protected, where our voice can be heard no matter how ugly it is, where a young coal miner's daughter can sing her heart out, and where an African-American boy can overcome stereotypes to become an iconic actor.

China

A photograph from my trip to Xi'an, China.

Being a photojournalist also results in several trips a year. One time I traveled to China for an assignment for *The Commission* magazine of the Southern Baptist Convention. I arrived in Xi'an (Pronounced: Shian) and was like a boy in a candy store. The place was exotic, and every corner demanded a photograph. I met nice people that fed me and offered for me to stay with them. One of those I met was a man about thirty years old whose name was Chan Cui (A beautiful Jade), and who wanted to know everything about me.

My assignment was to do a story on the sixty thousand Muslim Chinese who live in Xi'an. They are considered a minority, so they enjoy a few less perks than normal Chinese citizens. I was given that assignment since I used to be Muslim, giving me access to areas forbidden to non-Muslims. I found the Muslim Chinese intriguing. They could not read Arabic, yet they read the Quran written in Arabic. They actually just mouthed the words. I asked them what certain passages meant, and they had no idea.

Chan asked me many questions and was interested in why I converted, and what it was about Christ that appealed to me. I shared with him as well as I could, then asked him what faith he claimed. He looked at me puzzled and said, "I am nothing."

I had read that most Chinese don't believe in God. They just believe in the *Way*, a morality that keeps them from doing wrong. Confucius (who lived in China from 551 to 479 BC) coined the principle when he encouraged good conduct based on humanity and doing the right thing for the sake of goodness.

I had just read *Mere Christianity* by C. S. Lewis, and I shared a quote with Chan Cui: "The Christian is in a different position from other people who are trying to be good. They hope, by being good, to please God if there is one; or—if they think there is not—at least they hope to deserve approval from good men. But the Christian thinks any good he does comes from the Christ-life inside him. *He does not think God will love us because we are good, but that God will make us good because He loves us*; just as the roof of a greenhouse does not attract the sun because it is bright, but becomes bright because the sun shines on it."

Chan looked at the quote and became very quiet. Then he said, "But why does religion cause all these wars?" I tried to explain to him that the opposite happens when you truly believe. He remained convinced that his way is better. I saw Chan a few more times, and every time he would ask me questions about Christ, and I would share with him Bible verses.

The story was taking shape, and I met sweet Muslim Chinese families. I never shared my conversion with them out of respect. The ones that asked, I would say I was Christian. Then a few that knew about *Karim* being a name for God in Islam asked. With those I shared my story. They were respectful, but I could tell they were disappointed. This was during the time when Christ was not my Savior, so I did not feel like being a missionary. I regret losing that chance. I lost track of Chan after that trip, and I wondered what happened to him.

I wondered about the most populace country on earth with over a billion people, and how it came to be full of nonbelievers. I also wondered about the freedoms they lack. The country lags far behind when it comes to human rights. They have issues with freedom in the press, rights of laborers, and freedom of religion – highlighted by the repression of Christianity.

Americans need to look up to the heavens and thank God they were born in a free country that does not dictate beliefs, actions, sayings, or thoughts on its people. I am thankful my children are growing up in a country that respects their freedom and their citizenship. And I pray that these freedoms will not be removed.

My Children

My three children in their youth

"So in Christ Jesus you are all children of God through faith."
Galatians 3:26

I am ecstatic that freedom is all my children have ever known. And I make sure they never take it for granted, as I am always comparing their days with days of my youth. They have heard so many stories, now they just look at me rolling their eyes and say, "We know Daaaaaaad!"

Zade aspires to be a lawyer. He is heading towards politics and I applaud his perseverance through his challenging and well-crafted college classes. Dury is a music lover who is on the competitive snare drumline at school. And Demi is my angel who sings like a pro and has dreams of stardom. I am so blessed with my children, and I pray for them daily that they never overlook what they have here: opportunity, liberty, and a fair shake.

Zade is an intelligent young man. When he talks about social justice or a constitutional law paper he is writing, he is over my head within minutes. I have to always ask him to repeat his train of thoughts. He had me proofread a few of his papers, and I am ashamed to say I had to read them several times. He is a handsome fellow with black hair and a pretty smile, and he is very strong. He is funny and lovable and can make a joke out of anything. But his brain is what I love the most. He knows the latest regarding most countries. He reads a lot and is versatile. I spend hours with him talking about politics, social issues, history, law... etc. He reminds me of the hours I spent talking to my dad when I was his age.

Next in line is Dury, the one I want to embrace. He is truly a beautiful boy. He has curly brown hair that used to be blonde and bright. His cheeks are made for squeezing, and his eyes are blue with long eyelashes. He is funny and adorable, and girls hang around him like bees on honey. Dury has the skill to master anything he puts his mind to. One year he saw a guy flick a playing card about twenty feet. He started practicing and soon enough, he could flick it thirty and forty feet. Then he saw someone assemble the Rubik's Cube, and within a month he mastered it. And music, wow, he can play any instrument, and I mean any instrument. He plays the drums for band, but he can play the guitar, the trumpet, the base, and the saxophone; he can make music with anything you put in his hands. He wants to study music education.

The youngest is Demi Sunshine. She is my precious girl, and I cannot get enough of her wit and lovable personality. She is such a youngest child - she can charm people into doing anything for her, and is happy all the time. She has greenish-blue eyes and long brown hair and is slim and fit. She sang a solo every year at her school talent show, always receiving a standing ovation. She teaches me how to sing in the car. She will sing: tra la la at a certain pitch. I try to repeat using the exact pitch, sometimes I hit it, but mostly I miss. She will say: "That was a half note too sharp." *Half a note?* I am lucky if I can detect the pitch within two or three notes! She has so many friends and is the life of the party. She is loved by all of them. I can't do Lilly Lilly the caterpillar anymore since she is a teenager. I used to hold my pointer finger and act as if it was a caterpillar; she would hold it and love on it and laugh with it. But now if I attempt to bring him out, she will look at me and say, "Really dad . . . I am a teenager now." She loves the sound of the word *teenager*.

Zade outgrew Lilly Lilly in fifth grade, but Dury was five years old and he still loved him. So Lilly Lilly stayed around. Dury would look at my finger and say, "Alligator," and Lilly Lilly, or my finger, would shake and scream. Well, I was doing the screaming. Then Lilly Lilly would try to hide in Dury's tummy while tickling him. This went on for years, then Dury reached fifth grade and sure enough, he informed me that he was done with Lilly Lilly. My finger was very sad that day except for Demi was next in line. She loved Lilly Lilly and would introduce him to her friends at preschool. He told stories, and he would build a shield around him to keep safe. Demi would spray him with a "Take Down the Shield Spray" and then she would scare him with "Lion" or "Bear." Lilly Lilly would scream and tickle her. This went on for years until, you guessed right: fifth grade. She looked at me one day when I whipped him out and said, "No dad." Lilly Lilly was crushed. There were no more children to play with, and he was old and grumpy. He was born when Zade was born. I don't know what twenty-one is in caterpillar years! Now Lilly Lilly comes out only to embarrass them and to threaten that he is coming to their wedding to make a toast!

Life in this country provides for moments like these to bloom no matter how silly they may seem. Basic necessities are reasonably attained, like food and water and a roof over your head. This leaves room for the imagination to play and for actions of diligence, devotion, and determination to blossom. Everything I do, I view from a window letting in the freedom we ought to cherish every day, and I dream with that window open.

Thanks for the Risk Takers

Many people helped me along my twelve-year journey to Christ, and I am forever in their debt. They took a risk deciding to mentor me and explain the Gospel to me. They did not stay in the comfort zone of never-talking-about-religion-with-anyone. They pushed through and shared with me what amounted to little steps along the path to finding Christ. Gil, Frank, and Dana were instrumental, but there were others that had their share.

The first to come to mind was my photography teacher at the University of Tennessee, Rob Heller. Rob was the first Jewish person I knew. He liked me and helped me pursue photography into a career. I admire Rob for teaching an Arab without any prejudice or hate.

Next would be Bill Bangham, who is the Director of Media Production, The International Mission Board of The Southern Baptist Convention. Bill's answer to many of my questions was: "God loves you, Karim." This was at a time when I was searching and did not understand that it was all about love. Bill would be the one who introduced me to love as Christ intended it to be, love between brothers, and love between man and God. His talks were always soft and non-judgmental.

Another wonderful brother in the Lord is John Constantine. The pastor with the Arabic Baptist Church of Birmingham, which meets at Dawson Baptist Church. I have had two major "aha" moments based on John's preaching: one about self-denial, the other about obedience which leads to faith. These thoughts have been encouraging me ever since I heard them.

Another person was Jesse Palmer, a man who hired me for photography and spent a lot of time teaching and leading me to Christ. Others who planted seeds were Aubrey Miller, Tim Simmons, Andy Wolfe, Todd Harrington, Bill King, Monier Emaish, Scott Myers, and many other brothers in Christ.

I will always think of them as people who supported my journey, no matter if it took twelve years!

Freedom of Religion/Freedom in Christ

While freedom of religion is precious and a gift never to be trifled, infinitely more precious is the freedom and citizenship in Christ. Jesus truly sets us free not only to worship God, but to burgeon as human beings who care for, and love this entire world – a burden encouraged in Christ. Freedom in Christ is not obtained, Jesus himself gives it to us. We are free because of His sacrifice on the Cross. Charles Wesley captures the Christian experience of this liberation in one of his great hymns:

Long my imprisoned spirit lay
Fast bound in sin and nature's night;
Thine eye diffused a quickening ray,
I woke, the dungeon flamed with light.
My chains fell off, my heart was free;
I rose, went forth, and followed thee.

And Saint Paul puts it best in Galatians 5:1:

"For freedom Christ has set us free; stand firm therefore, and do not submit again to a yoke of slavery." Christ sets us free from slavery to the law and to whatever is holding us hostage. All we have to do is believe in Him, and accept His gorgeous freedom.

I do pray my children and all of the children of this country and the world learn about this freedom and citizenship in Christ. I pray the words of Saint Paul resonate within the deepest crevices of their souls. I pray the thumping of their heart grows vehement as they listen to those words. I finally pray they know the difference between man-made freedom, and heavenly freedom in Christ. We have to open our hearts and minds and accept His sacrifice for the redemption of our sins.

Indeed, we can be free in Christ always. Saint Paul wrote about joy, love, peace, and freedom from the dark dungeon of a jail cell:

"About midnight Paul and Silas were praying and singing hymns to God, and the prisoners were listening to them,. . ." Acts 16:25

Suffering and trials seemed to motivate the Apostle Paul to live more joyfully and freely as his citizenship was in a kingdom not of this world. During another imprisonment, he writes:

"For the sake of Christ, then, I am content with weaknesses, insults, hardships, persecutions, and calamities. For when I am weak, then I am strong." 2 Corinthians 12:10

Freedom in Christ lights up even the darkest place. It shines where nothing else can shine, and it takes us from depressive states to effervescent realms. Freedom in Christ can and will transform our life from dull to bright, from drab to beautiful, and from dim to brilliant.

Living in America has allowed me to become a Christian without fear of any punishment or persecution. I can't say the same about other countries. Religion is closely monitored and forced on people in many places. The beauty of freedom escapes millions of believers who live under scrutiny and persecution in other parts of this vast world. And while my path to Christianity was long and circuitous, there were many points along the way where I learned about a precise and definite proof that Christianity is not only the way, but the truth and the life as well.

Your Journey

"Now may the Lord of peace himself give you peace at all times in every way. The Lord be with you all." 2 Thessalonians 3:16

_____

_____

_____

_____

_____

_____

_____

_____

_____

_____

_____

_____

_____

_____

_____

_____

The Great Fight of Faith
by J. Gresham Machen

The Apostle Paul was a great fighter. His fighting was partly against external enemies—against hardships of all kinds. Five times he was scourged by the Jews, three times by the Romans; he suffered shipwreck four times; and was in perils of waters, in perils of robbers, in perils by his own countrymen, in perils by the heathen, in perils in the city, in perils in the wilderness, in perils in the sea, in perils among false brethren. And finally he came to the logical end of such a life, by the headsman's axe. It was hardly a peaceful life, but was rather a life of wild adventure. Charles Lindbergh, I suppose, got a thrill when he hopped off to Paris, and people are in search of thrills today; but if you wanted a really unbroken succession of thrills, I think you could hardly do better than try knocking around the Roman Empire of the first century with the Apostle Paul, engaged in the unpopular business of turning the world upside down.

But these physical hardships were not the chief battle in which Paul was engaged. Far more trying was the battle that he fought against the enemies in his own camp. Everywhere his rear was threatened by an all-engulfing paganism or by a perverted Judaism that has missed the real purpose of the Old Testament law. Read the Epistles with care, and you see Paul always in conflict. At one time he fights paganism in life, the notion that all kinds of conduct are lawful to the Christian man, a philosophy that makes Christian liberty a mere aid to pagan license. At another time, he fights paganism in thought, the sublimation of the Christian doctrine of the resurrection of the body into the pagan doctrine of the immortality of the soul. At still another time, he fights the effort of human pride to substitute man's merit as the means of salvation for divine grace; he fights the subtle propaganda of the Judaizers with its misleading appeal to the Word of God. Everywhere we see the great apostle in conflict for the preservation of the church. It is as though a mighty flood were seeking to engulf the church's life; dam the break at one point in the levee, and another break appears somewhere else. Everywhere paganism was seeping through; not for one moment did Paul have peace; always he was called upon to fight.

Fortunately, he was a true fighter; and by God's grace he not only fought, but he won. At first sight indeed he might have seemed to have lost. The lofty doctrine of divine grace, the center and core of the gospel that Paul preached, did not always dominate the mind and heart of the subsequent church. The Christianity of the Apostolic Fathers, of the Apologists, of Irenæus, is very different from the Christianity of Paul. The church meant to be faithful to the apostle; but the pure doctrine of the Cross runs counter to the natural man, and not always, even in the church, was it fully understood. Read the Epistle to the Romans first, and then read Irenæus, and you are conscious of a mighty decline. No longer does the gospel stand out sharp and clear; there is a large admixture of human error; and it might seem as though Christian freedom, after all, were to be entangled in the meshes of a new law.

But even Irenæus is very different from the Judaizers; something had been gained even in his day: and God had greater things than Irenæus in store for the church. The Epistles which Paul struck forth in conflict with the opponents in his own day remained in the New Testament as a personal source of life for the people of God. Augustine on the basis of the Epistles, set forth the Pauline doctrine of sin and grace; and then, after centuries of compromise with the natural man, the Reformation rediscovered the great liberating Pauline doctrine of justification by faith. So it has always been with Paul. Just when he seems to be defeated, his greatest triumphs, by God's grace, are in store.

The human instruments, however, which God uses in great triumphs of faith are no pacifists, but great fighters like Paul himself. Little affinity for the great apostle has the whole tribe of considerers of consequences, the whole tribe of the compromisers ancient and modern. The real companions of Paul are the great heroes of the faith. But who are those heroes? Are they not true fighters, one and all? Tertullian fought a mighty battle against Marcion; Athanasius fought against the Arians; Augustine fought against Pelagius; and as for Luther, he fought a brave battle against kings and princes and popes for the liberty of the people of God. Luther was a great fighter; and we love him for it. So was Calvin; so were John Knox and all the rest. It is impossible to be a true soldier of Jesus Christ and not fight.

God grant that you...may be fighters, too! Probably you have your battles even now; you have to contend against sins gross or sins refined; you have to contend against the sin of slothfulness and inertia; you have, many of you, I know very well, a mighty battle on your hands against doubt and despair. Do not think it strange if you fall thus into divers temptations. The Christian life is a warfare after all. John Bunyan rightly set it forth under the allegory of a Holy War; and when he set it forth, in his greater book, under the figure of a pilgrimage, the pilgrimage, too, was full of battles. There are, indeed, places of refreshment on the Christian way; the House Beautiful was provided by the King at the top of the Hill Difficulty, for the entertainment of pilgrims, and from the Delectable Mountains could sometimes be discerned the shining towers of the City of God. But just after the descent from the House Beautiful, there was the battle with Apollyon and the Valley of Humiliation, and later came the Valley of the Shadow of Death. No, the Christian faces a mighty conflict in this world. Pray God that in that conflict you may be true men; good soldiers of Jesus Christ, not willing to compromise with your great enemy, not easily cast down, and seeking ever the renewing of your strength in the Word and sacraments and prayer!

You will have a battle, too, when you go forth as ministers into the church. The church is now in a period of deadly conflict. The redemptive religion known as Christianity is contending, in our own Presbyterian Church and in all the larger churches in the world, against a totally alien type of religion. As always, the enemy conceals his most dangerous assaults under pious phrases and half truths. The shibboleths of the adversary have sometimes a very deceptive sound. "Let us propagate Christianity," the adversary says, "but let us not always be engaged in arguing in defense of it; let us make our preaching positive, and not negative; let us avoid controversy; let us hold to a Person and not to dogma; let us sink small doctrinal differences and seek the unity of the church of Christ; let us drop doctrinal accretions and interpret Christ for ourselves; let us look for our knowledge of Christ in our hearts; let us not impose Western creeds on the Eastern mind; let us be tolerant of opposing views." Such are some of the shibboleths of that agnostic Modernism which is the deadliest enemy of the Christian religion to-day. They deceive some of God's people some of the time; they are heard sometimes from the lips of good Christian people, who have not the slightest inkling of what they mean. But their true meaning, to thinking men, is becoming increasingly clear. Increasingly it is becoming necessary for a man to decide whether he is going to stand or not to stand for the Lord Jesus Christ as he is presented to us in the Word of God.

If you decide to stand for Christ, you will not have an easy life in the ministry. Of course, you may try to evade the conflict. All men will speak well of you if, after preaching no matter how unpopular a Gospel on Sunday, you will only vote against that Gospel in the councils of the church the next day; you will graciously be permitted to believe in supernatural Christianity all you please if you will only act as though you did not believe in it, if you will only make common cause with its opponents. Such is the program that will win the favor of the church. A man may believe what he pleases, provided he does not believe anything strongly enough to risk his life on it and fight for it. "Tolerance" is the great word. Men even ask for tolerance when they look to God in prayer. But how can any Christian possibly pray such a prayer as that? What a terrible prayer it is, how full of disloyalty to the Lord Jesus Christ! There is a sense, of course, in which tolerance is a virtue. If by it you mean tolerance on the part of the state, the forbearance of majorities toward minorities, the resolute rejection of any measures of physical compulsion in propagating either what is true or what is false, then of course, the Christian ought to favor tolerance with all his might and main, and ought to lament the widespread growth of intolerance in America today. Or if you mean by tolerance forbearance toward personal attacks upon yourself, or courtesy and patience and fairness in dealing with all errors of whatever kind, then again tolerance is a virtue. But to pray for tolerance apart from such qualifications, in particular to pray for tolerance without careful definition of that of which you are to be tolerant, is just to pray for the breakdown of the Christian religion; for the Christian religion is intolerant to the core. There lies the whole offense of the Cross—and also the whole power of it. Always the Gospel would have been received with favor by the world IF it had been presented merely as one way of salvation; the offense came because it was presented as the only way, and because it made relentless war upon all other ways. God save us, then, from this "tolerance" of which we hear so much : God deliver us from the sin of making common cause with those who deny or ignore the blessed Gospel of Jesus Christ! God save us from the deadly guilt of consenting to the presence as our representatives in the church of those who lead Christ's little ones astray; God make us, whatever else we are, just faithful messengers, who present, without fear or favor, not our word, but the Word of God.

But if you are such messengers, you will have the opposition, not only of the world, but increasingly, I fear, of the Church. I cannot tell you that your sacrifice will be light. No doubt it would be noble to care nothing whatever about the judgment of our fellowmen. But to such nobility I confess that I for my part have not quite attained, and I cannot expect you to have attained to it. I confess that academic preferments, easy access to great libraries, the society of cultured people, and in general the thousand advantages that come from being regarded as respectable people in a respectable world—I confess that these things seem to me to be in themselves good and desirable things. Yet the servant of Jesus Christ, to an increasing extent, is being obliged to give them up. Certainly, in making that sacrifice we do not complain; for we have something with which all that we have lost is not worthy to be compared. Still, it can hardly be said that any unworthy motives of self-interest can lead us to adopt a course which brings us nothing but reproach. Where, then, shall we find a sufficient motive for such a course as that; where shall we find courage to stand against the whole current of the age; where shall we find courage for this fight of faith?

I do not think that we shall obtain courage by any mere lust of conflict. Perhaps it may be necessary in some kinds of war. But it will hardly serve in this Christian conflict. In this conflict I do not think we can be good fighters simply by being resolved to fight. For this battle is a battle of love; and nothing ruins a man's service in it so much as a spirit of hate.

No, if we want to learn the secret of this warfare, we shall have to look deeper; and we can hardly do better than turn again to that great fighter, the Apostle Paul. What was the secret of his power in the mighty conflict; how did he learn to fight?

The answer is paradoxical; but it is very simple. Paul was a great fighter because he was at peace. He who said, "Fight the good fight of faith," spoke also of "the peace of God which passeth all understanding"; and in that peace the sinews of his war were found. He fought against the enemies that were without because he was at peace within; there was an inner sanctuary in his life that no enemy could disturb. There, my friends, is the great central truth. You cannot fight successfully with beasts, as Paul did at Ephesus; you cannot fight successfully against evil men, or against the devil and his spiritual powers of wickedness in high places, unless when you fight against those enemies there is One with whom you are at peace.

But if you are at peace with that One, then you can care little what men may do. You can say with the apostles, "We must obey God rather than men"; you can say with Luther, "Here I stand, I cannot do otherwise, God help me. Amen"; you can say with Elisha, "They that be with us are more than they that be with them"; you can say with Paul, "It is God that justifieth, who is he that condemneth?" Without that peace of God in your hearts, you will strike little terror into the enemies of the Gospel of Christ. You may amass mighty resources for the conflict; you may be great masters of ecclesiastical strategy; you may be very clever, and very zealous too; but I fear that it will be of little avail. There may be a tremendous din; but when the din is over, the Lord's enemies will be in possession of the field. No, there is no other way to be a really good fighter. You cannot fight God's battle against God's enemies unless you are at peace with him.

But how shall you be at peace with him? Many ways have been tried. How pathetic is the age-long effort of sinful man to become right with God; sacrifice, lacerations, almsgiving, morality, penance, confession! But alas, it is all of no avail. Still there is that same awful gulf. It may be temporarily concealed; spiritual exercises may conceal it for a time; penance or the confession of sin unto men may give a temporary and apparent relief. But the real trouble remains; the burden is still on the back; Mount Sinai is still ready to shoot forth flames; the soul is still not at peace with God. How then shall peace be obtained?

My friends, it cannot be attained by anything in us. Oh, that that truth could be written in the hearts of every one of you! If it could be written in the hearts of every one of you, the main purpose of this seminary would be attained. Oh, that it could be written in letters of flame for all the world to read! Peace with God cannot be attained by any act or any mere experience of man; it cannot be attained by good works, neither can it be attained by confession of sin, neither can it be attained by any psychological results of an act of faith. We can never be at peace with God unless God first be at peace with us. But how can God be at peace with us? Can he be at peace with us by ignoring the guilt of sin? by descending from his throne? by throwing the universe into chaos? by making wrong to be the same as right? by making a dead letter of his holy law? "The soul that sinneth it shall die," by treating his eternal laws as though they were the changeable laws of man? Oh, what an abyss were the universe if that were done, what a mad anarchy, what a wild demon-riot! Where could there be peace if God were thus at war with himself; where could there be a foundation if God's laws were not sure? Oh, no, my friends, peace cannot be attained for man by the great modern method of dragging God down to man's level; peace cannot be attained by denying that right is right and wrong is wrong; peace can nowhere be attained if the awful justice of God stand not forever sure.

How then can we sinners stand before that throne? How can there be peace for us in the presence of the justice of God? How can he be just and yet justify the ungodly? There is one answer to these questions. It is not our answer. Our wisdom could never have discovered it. It is God's answer. It is found in the story of the Cross. We deserved eternal death because of sin; the eternal Son of God, because he loved us, and because he was sent by the Father who loved us too, died in our stead, for our sins, upon the cross. That message is despised to-day; upon it the visible church as well as the world pours out the vials of its scorn, or else does it even less honor by paying it lip-service and then passing it by. Men dismiss it as a "theory of the atonement," and fall back upon the customary commonplaces about a principle of self-sacrifice, or the culmination of a universal law, or a revelation of the love of God, or the hallowing of suffering, or the similarity between Christ's death and the death of soldiers who perished in the great war. In the presence of such blindness, our words often seem vain. We may tell men something of what we think about the Cross of Christ, but it is harder to tell them what we feel. We pour forth our tears of gratitude and love; we open to the multitude the depths of our souls; we celebrate a mystery so tender, so holy, that we might think it would soften even a heart of stone. But all to no purpose. The Cross remains foolishness to the world, men turn coldly away, and our preaching seems but vain. And then comes the wonder of wonders! The hour comes for some poor soul, even through the simplest and poorest preaching; the message is honored, not the messenger; there comes a flash of light into the soul, and all is as clear as day. "He loved me and gave Himself for me," says the sinner at last, as he contemplates the Savior upon the Cross. The burden of sin falls from the back, and a soul enters into the peace of God.

Have you yourselves that peace, my friends? If you have, you will not be deceived by the propaganda of any disloyal church. If you have the peace of God in your hearts, you will never shrink from controversy; you will never be afraid to contend earnestly for the Faith. Talk of peace in the present deadly peril of the Church, and you show, unless you be strangely ignorant of the conditions that exist, that you have little inkling of the true peace of God. Those who have been at the foot of the Cross will not be afraid to go forth under the banner of the Cross to a holy war of love.

Many of you are called upon to pass through deep waters and to face fiery trials. Never is it an easy process to substitute for the unthinking faith of childhood the fire-tested convictions of full-grown men. But may God bring you through! May God bring you out from the mists of doubt and hesitation into the clear shining of the light of faith. You may not indeed at once attain full clearness; gloomy doubts may arise like angels of Satan to buffet you. But God grant that you may have sufficient clearness to stand at least for Jesus Christ. It will not be easy. Many have been swept from their moorings by the current of the age; a church grown worldly often tyrannizes over those who look for guidance to God's Word alone. But this is not the first discouraging time in the history of the church; other times were just as dark, and yet always God has watched over His people, and the darkest hour has sometimes preceded the dawn. So even now God has not left Himself without a witness. In many lands there are those who have faced the great issue of the day and have decided it aright, who have preserved true independence of mind in the presence of the world; in many lands there are groups of Christian people who in the face of ecclesiastical tyranny have not been afraid to stand for Jesus Christ. God grant that you may give comfort to them as you go forth from this seminary; God grant that you may rejoice their hearts by giving them your hand and your voice. To do so you will need courage. Far easier is it to curry favor with the world by abusing those whom the world abuses, by speaking against controversy, by taking a balcony view of the struggle in which God's servants are engaged. But God save you from such a neutrality as that! It has a certain worldly appearance of urbanity and charity. But how cruel it is to burdened souls; how heartless it is to those little ones who are looking to the Church for some clear message from God! God save you from being so heartless and so unloving and so cold! God grant, instead, that in all humility but also in all boldness, in reliance upon God, you may fight the good fight of faith. Peace is indeed yours, the peace of God which passeth all understanding. But that peace is given you, not that you may be onlookers or neutrals in love's battle, but that you may be good soldiers of Jesus Christ.

CHAPTER TEN

Why My Conversion Is the Most Reasonable Action I Have Ever Taken

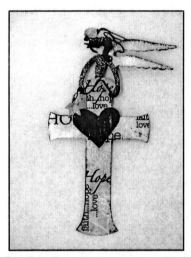

Frank and Barbara Barker gave me this Cross.

"Now I would remind you, brothers, of the gospel I preached to you, which you received, in which you stand, and by which you are being saved, if you hold fast to the word I preached to you—unless you believed in vain. For I delivered to you as of first importance what I also received: that Christ died for our sins in accordance with the Scriptures, that he was buried, that he was raised on the third day in accordance with the Scriptures, and that he appeared to Cephas, then to the twelve. Then he appeared to more than five hundred brothers at one time, most of whom are still alive, though some have fallen asleep. Then he appeared to James, then to all the apostles. Last of all, as to one untimely born, he appeared also to me. For I am the least of the apostles, unworthy to be called an apostle, because I persecuted the church of God. But by the grace of God I am what I am, and his grace toward me was not in vain. On the contrary, I worked harder than any of them, though it was not I, but the grace of God that is with me. Whether then it was I or they, so we preach and so you believed." 1 Corinthians 15:1-11

It took me twelve years to believe in the true Christ and to live in partnership with His Holy Spirit. It was my personal stubbornness and unwillingness to submit to Christ, as the only and sufficient way of Salvation, that kept me in the darkness for a long time. I know we operate on His time, yet my unbelief was inexcusable. And since I became a true believer in 2008, I have delved into the Bible and other books by Christian writers, and I have found many reasons why Christianity is *the* way to God. Apologetics is not one of my strong areas of Biblical knowledge, but I must lay out the substantiation I found during my research. Anyone disputing the fact that Jesus Christ is the way, the truth, and the life, needs to examine the evidence:

1 – Prophecies:

The Old Testament was completed four hundred years before the birth of Christ. It contains verses predicting Christ's birth, life, death, and Resurrection. These verses coincide with the New Testament to a staggering degree. According to the J. Barton Payne's *Encyclopedia of Biblical Prophecy*, "*There are 1,239 prophecies in the Old Testament.*" Here are a few:

- **Christ was Born of a Virgin**

Isaiah 7:14: "*Therefore the Lord himself will give you a sign. Behold, the virgin shall conceive and bear a son, and shall call his name Immanuel.*"

- **Christ is the Son of God**

Psalm 2:7: "*I will tell of the decree: The Lord said to me, 'You are my Son; today I have begotten you.'*"

- **Born at Bethlehem**

Micah 5:2: "*But you, Bethlehem Ephrathah, though you are small among the clans of Judah, out of you will come for me one who will be ruler over Israel, whose origins are from of old, from ancient times.*"

- His Side Pierced

Zechariah 12:10: *"And I will pour out on the house of David and the inhabitants of Jerusalem a spirit of grace and supplication. They will look on me, the one they have pierced, and they will mourn for him as one mourns for an only child, and grieve bitterly for him as one mourns for an only son."*

- The Crucifixion

Psalm 22:1, 11-18: *"My God, my God, why have you forsaken me? Do not be far from me, for trouble is near and there is no one to help. Many bulls surround me; strong bulls of Bashan. Dogs have surrounded me; a band of evil men has encircled me, they have pierced my hands and my feet. I can count all my bones; people stare and gloat over me. They divide my garments among them and cast lots for my clothing."*

- The Resurrection

Psalm 16:10: *"Because you will not abandon me to the realm of the dead, nor will you let your faithful one see decay."*

- The following chapter contains many prophecies:

Isaiah 53: *"Who has believed our message and to whom has the arm of the Lord been revealed? He grew up before him like a tender shoot, and like a root out of dry ground. He had no beauty or majesty to attract us to him, nothing in his appearance that we should desire him. He was despised and rejected by mankind, a man of suffering, and familiar with pain. Like one from whom people hide their faces he was despised, and we held him in low esteem. Surely he took up our pain and bore our suffering, yet we considered him punished by God, stricken by him, and afflicted.*

But he was pierced for our transgressions, he was crushed for our iniquities; the punishment that brought us peace was on him, and by his wounds we are healed.

We all, like sheep, have gone astray, each of us has turned to our own way; and the Lord has laid on him the iniquity of us all. He was oppressed and afflicted, yet he did not open his mouth; he was led like a lamb to the slaughter, and as a sheep before its shearers is silent, so he did not open his mouth. By oppression and judgment he was taken away. Yet who of his generation protested? For he was cut off from the land of the living; for the transgression of my people he was punished. He was assigned a grave with the wicked, and with the rich in his death, though he had done no violence, nor was any deceit in his mouth. Yet it was the Lord's will to crush him and cause him to suffer, and though the Lord makes his life an offering for sin, he will see his offspring and prolong his days, and the will of the Lord will prosper in his hand. After he has suffered, he will see the light of life and be satisfied; by his knowledge my righteous servant will justify many, and he will bear their iniquities. Therefore I will give him a portion among the great, and he will divide the spoils with the strong, because he poured out his life unto death, and was numbered with the transgressors.

For he bore the sin of many, and made intercession for the transgressors."

How did all these Old Testament writers know about Jesus and His birth, life, death, and Resurrection? The only way I can explain it is prophecy. God raised up men as prophets and revealed to them things that would happen in the future, and urged them to write it down as a testimony for all.

2 – The Bible is True:

The Gospel of Luke begins:

"Inasmuch as many have undertaken to compile a narrative of the things that have been accomplished among us, just as those who from the beginning were eyewitnesses and ministers of the word have delivered them to us, it seemed good to me also, having followed all things closely for some time past, to write an orderly account for you, most excellent Theophilus, that you may have certainty concerning the things you have been taught." Luke 1:1-4

Luke tells us he is chronicling the events in sequence. He also states that he examined the events and is documenting it so that we may know the truth. He uses words like, "eye witnesses, investigated, and exact truth." This is not an accidental presupposition. This is a well-researched treatise with strong evidence behind it. Besides, Luke was not the only one writing from that period.

The Jewish historian Josephus, wrote for the Roman Government in 70 AD. He confirmed that John the Baptist died at the hands of Herod (this same incident is recorded in the Gospels); as well as the death of *"The brother of Jesus, who was called Christ, whose name was James. . . he delivered them to be stoned"* (Josephus, Antiquities of the Jews, Book XVIII, ch. V, p. 20; Book XX, ch. IX, p. 140). This is external evidence confirming the existence of Jesus and His disciples.

Josephus also tells of how the Jews copied the Old Testament. *"We have given practical proof of our reverence for our own Scriptures. For although such long ages have now passed, no one has ventured either to add, or to remove, or to alter a syllable; and it is an instinct with every Jew, from the day of his birth, to regard them as the decrees of God, to abide by them, and, if need be, cheerfully to die for them"* (Against Apion, Book I, sec., 8, p. 158).

The discovery of the Dead Sea Scrolls in 1947 shed further light upon the tremendous accuracy of the transmission of the biblical documents over time. Before this discovery, the earliest Hebrew texts we possessed were from the 10th century. Some of the biblical materials found in the Dead Sea Scrolls (DSS) could possibly be as old as 250 B.C., and at least as early as 100 B.C. The Isaiah scroll from the DSS is identical in almost all details to the Massoretic text from a thousand years later, showing that it is not necessary to conclude that all written texts will be corrupted over time. Other biblical finds from the DSS show other lines of transmission, such as that found in the Greek version of the Old Testament, the Septuagint.

And we have a similar pattern in the New Testament with over five thousand Greek manuscripts in existence. Josh McDowell puts it best in his book, *Evidence of the Resurrection:*

"Because the New Testament provides the primary historical source for information on the resurrection, many critics during the 19th century attacked the reliability of these biblical documents. By the end of the 19th century, however, archaeological discoveries had confirmed the accuracy of the New Testament manuscripts. Discoveries of early papyri bridged the gap between the time of Christ and existing manuscripts from a later date. Those findings increased

scholarly confidence in the reliability of the Bible. William F. Al-bright, who in his day was the world's foremost biblical archaeol-ogist said: 'We can already say emphatically that there is no lon-ger any solid basis for dating any book of the New Testament after about A.D. 80, two full generations before the date between 130 and 150 given by the more radical New Testament critics of today.'

Josh McDowell continues, *"Coinciding with the papyri discov-eries, an abundance of other manuscripts came to light (over 24,000 copies of early New Testament manuscripts are known to be in exis-tence today). The historian Luke wrote of 'authentic evidence' con-cerning the resurrection. Sir William Ramsay, who spent 15 years attempting to undermine Luke's credentials as a historian, and to refute the reliability of the New Testament, finally concluded: 'Luke is a historian of the first rank . . . This author should be placed along with the very greatest of historians.'*

If the Bible were made up, it would have taken a miracle to organize what forty writers documented over the period of fif-teen hundred years and have it tell the story of God's redemption of mankind through Jesus Christ. In addition, the only thing that these men gained from what they wrote was death.

3 – Resurrection:

According to Jewish customs, the body of Jesus was wrapped in Linen and then one hundred pounds of spices were adminis-tered to the wrappings. After that he was placed in a tomb, and a large rock (weighing approximately two tons) was rolled to cover the door. A Roman guard was assigned to the tomb, which was also sealed by a Roman seal not to be broken. Three days later, His followers said that Jesus rose from the dead. Paul mentions that he appeared to five hundred followers at one time. Consider these facts surrounding the Resurrection:

– **A broken Roman seal:** The punishment for breaking a Roman seal was execution by crucifixion upside down. That is a big risk to take just to steal a body.

– **The empty tomb:** The disciples did not go far but stayed close to the tomb preaching the Resurrection. It had to be true, otherwise they would be found to be liars had the body been found. Josh McDowell again, *"Paul Maier observes that ' . . . if all the evidence is weighed carefully and fairly, it is indeed justifiable, according to the canons of historical research, to conclude that the sepulcher of Joseph of Arimathea, in which Jesus was buried, was actually empty on the morning of the first Easter. And no shred of evidence has yet been discovered in literary sources, epigraphy, or archaeology that would disprove this statement.'"*

– **The linens:** John describes the linens covering the body left neatly in the grave. Why did it stick in his mind? Because it tells the story of someone leaving the grave on their own, as opposed to someone stealing the body and leaving the linens in a mess. And why would they leave the linens in the first place?

– **The appearance of Jesus confirmed by over five hundred people according to the Apostle Paul.**

Josh McDowell illustrates, *"Professor Thomas Arnold, for 14 years a headmaster of Rugby, author of the famous* History of Rome, *and appointed to the chair of modern history at Oxford, was well acquainted with the value of evidence in determining historical facts. This great scholar said: 'I have been used for many years to study the histories of other times, and to examine and weigh the evidence of those who have written about them, and I know of no one fact in the history of mankind which is proved by better and fuller evidence of every sort, to the understanding of a fair inquirer, than the great sign which God hath given us that Christ died and rose again from the dead.'"*

Brooke Foss Westcott, an English scholar, said, *"Raking all the evidence together, it is not too much to say that there is no historic incident better or more variously supported than the resurrection of Christ. Nothing but the antecedent assumption that it must be false could have suggested the idea of deficiency in the proof of it."*

The most revealing evidence is what happened to the disciples. What caused them to go around spreading the tale if it were not true? They were beaten, crucified, thrown to lions, and stoned to death. What would drive them to live that life if there were no Resurrection? Or perhaps the better question is: Why would someone give his life up for a lie?

4 – The Quran Considers Him a Miracle:

Considering I converted from Islam, I have the desire to explain to Muslims in particular the stature of Jesus in their holy book, the Quran:

Christ holds the highest stature in the Quran, which mentions Jesus by name twenty-five times. He did not only perform miracles, but He himself was a miracle - He was born of a virgin mother, *"She said: 'O my Lord! How shall I have a son when no man hath touched me?' He said: 'Even so: Allah createth what He willeth: when He hath decreed a Plan He but saith to it, "Be," and it is!'" (Quran, al-Imran 3:47)* He is also considered to have performed many miracles: *"And We gave unto Jesus, son of Mary, clear miracles" (Quran, Al-Baqra 2:87).*

Some of those miracles were healing the blind and the leper, and raising the dead, *". . . And I heal those born blind, and the lepers, and I quicken the dead, by Allah's leave." (Al-Imran 3:49).* It also says: *"... and I bring to life the dead, by the permission of God." (Quran 3:49)*

What the Quran says about Jesus might be a starting point to start exploring Christianity. I pray if God is calling you, my Muslim friend, towards His ultimate redemption and Salvation, that you answer the call. Start by reading the book of John in the New Testament. Then read the Gospels of Matthew, Mark, and Luke. Seek the counsel of a close Christian friend and visit a church. Fellowship with brothers in Christ. I pray you are led to the wonderous path towards His Glory, and towards His Salvation.

Dr. James White is a leading apologist who has debated with numerous Muslim Imams. He says this about the Muslim view of

Salvation in his book, *What Every Christian Needs to Know About the Qur'an*:

> *"We want to ask, 'Does the Quran present a single, coherent view of Salvation?' But perhaps the more incisive question is whether the doctrine of Salvation is distinguishable from proper worship, the embracing of tawhid (The oneness of Allah), and the rejection of shirk (Association of someone with Allah), i.e. submission to Allah. It is easy for Christians to transport concepts derived from the biblical text into the Quran, but such will inevitably lead to miss-understanding, for while the Quranic and biblical worldviews share certain foundational assumptions, they are worlds apart regarding other definitional beliefs. The transcendence of Alllah, especially as put in direct opposition to the incarnation of Jesus and the intimacy of the Gospel, creates a stark contrast as to the respective meanings of 'Salvation'. The triune God of the Christian faith reveals Himself with greatest clarity and force in the Gospel (the Father decreeing, the Son accomplishing, the Spirit applying) while maintaining the strictest unity (the Son does nothing by himself, the Spirit is sent by the Father and the Son), so it can be said that His self-revelation is accomplished through the uniting of a particular undeserving people in grace to Him through the Gospel. Salvation, central to His purpose in creation itself, hence is a focus of the biblical revelation. In contrast, Allah is not engaged in self-revelation or self-glorification in the matter of human Salvation, and there is no Gospel that gives a singular coherence to the Islamic perspective."*

5 – My Aneurism:

This piece of evidence is from my own life. My chances of surviving the ruptured aneurysm that exploded in my brain on April 8, 1992, were very low. I was in a coma for nearly a month, and it took several more months to recuperate. I remember being in therapy with people who were in wheelchairs for years. I prayed that I would start talking soon, and I did. I also prayed that I would start walking one day, and three months after the aneurysm I did. It is as if God was saying, *"I want you to tell my story of loving you. I want you to tell about my Son who died for all of mankind. And I want you to tell about His grace, Redemption and Salvation."*

Just like Paul was not the only person God spoke to, I am not the only survivor of a ruptured aneurysm. The difference in Paul's experience was that it led him to live for Christ:

> *"Yes, and I will continue to rejoice, for I know that through your prayers and God's provision of the Spirit of Jesus Christ what has happened to me will turn out for my deliverance. I eagerly expect and hope that I will in no way be ashamed, but will have sufficient courage so that now as always Christ will be exalted in my body, whether by life or by death. FOR TO ME, TO LIVE IS CHRIST AND TO DIE IS GAIN. If I am to go on living in the body, this will mean fruitful labor for me. Yet what shall I choose? I do not know! I am torn between the two: I desire to depart and be with Christ, which is better by far; but it is more necessary for you that I remain in the body. Convinced of this, I know that I will remain, and I will continue with all of you for your progress and joy in the faith." Philippians 1:18-25*

As far as my experience, I try to live for Christ. But considering my children and my humanity, I am reluctant to say "to die is gain." Just like Paul decided to stay to preach the Word, that is what I will do: live with Him in me, as much as I possibly can with the deluge of life's distractions. I am too weak to say, "I am now living like Paul, or more reasonably attainable, like Rev. Frank Barker, whose sole purpose in life is to live for Christ." The temptations and distractions of life set me far behind Frank Barker, and much farther behind Paul. Despite the daily failure, I am reminded that His blood washes the slate clean every time I fail and confess, that His Holy Spirit and power can and will dwell in me more and more the closer I get to Him through the Word. This is what differentiates Christianity from other faiths - our loving Father lives in us when we believe.

6 – Love:

The last piece of evidence is what drew me to Christianity in the first place - God's unconditional love.

The reason God became man and dwelt among us only to suffer and be crucified is the fact that He loves us.

The reason we were created in the first place is the fact that He loves us.

The reason God has given us a way to be redeemed from our sins through believing in His Son is the fact that He loves us.

The reason we can place our trust in Him and surrender to Him is the fact that He loves us.

The fact that the entire Christian faith is based on nothing but God's love is astounding, amazing, and astonishing:

> *"For God so loved the world, that he gave his only Son, that whoever believes in him should not perish but have eternal life. For God did not send his Son into the world to condemn the world, but in order that the world might be saved through him." John 3:16,17*

Jesus instructs us about this love:

> *"You shall love the Lord your God with all your heart and with all your soul and with all your strength and with all your mind, and your neighbor as yourself." Luke 10:27*

This is an extremely profound idea. How can we love with our hearts, souls, minds, and bodies? Can we even understand that love? Can we love each other that way? Humans fail in love and relationships because we are unable to love that kind of love on our own. However, when the Holy Spirit dwells in us, He can empower us to love such love. God himself will enable us to love with our hearts, souls, minds, and bodies.

This is the greatest piece of evidence for Christianity. No other religion on the face of the earth preaches this love. It actually not only preaches this love, it will make living this love possible, which is astounding, amazing, and astonishing!

Growing up as a Muslim, I never knew the love of God. I knew the love of my earthly father and my earthly family; but God? I was supposed to be afraid of Him. What a wonderful thing it is to love God instead of living in fear of Him. I want to shout it from the rooftops: You can LOVE God! We can only do this because He first loved us.

The Case for Christ

Another book I have read and loved is *The Case For Christ* by Lee Strobel, who has a Masters of Studies in Law degree from Yale Law School. He was an award-winning journalist at the *Chicago Tribune*, and today he is a teaching pastor at Willow Creek Community Church in Chicago. He was a skeptic, but through his studies, he ended up proving that Christ was who He said He was – The Son of God who came to this earth to redeem us.

What follows is a question and answer section taken from *The Case for Christ*, a book that Dr. D. James Kennedy has called, "The new standard among existing contemporary apologetics."

– Can the biographies of Jesus be trusted?
    Craig Blomberg, one of the country's foremost authorities on the topic, built a convincing case that they reflect eyewitness testimony and bear the unmistakable earmarks of accuracy.

– Were Jesus' biographies reliably preserved for us?
    World-class scholar Bruce Metzger said that compared with other ancient documents, there is an unprecedented number of New Testament manuscripts and that they can be dated extremely close to the original writings.

– Did Jesus fulfill the attributes of God?
    Prominent theologian D. A Carson points out that there are lots of evidence that Jesus exhibited the characteristics of deity including omniscience (all knowing), omnipresence

(all present), omnipotence (all powerful), eternality (all timeless), and immutability (all unchanging).

– Did Jesus, and Jesus alone, match the identity of the Messiah?

Hundreds of years before Jesus was born, prophets foretold the coming of the Messiah, or the Anointed One, who would redeem God's people. Against astronomical odds – Jesus and only Jesus throughout history, matched this prophetic fingerprint perfectly.

– Was Jesus' body really absent from the tomb?

William Lane Craig presented striking evidence that the enduring symbol of Easter – the vacant tomb of Jesus – was a historical reality. The empty grave is reported or implied in extremely early sources, Mark's Gospel and the 1 Corinthians 15 creed.

– Was Jesus seen alive after His death on the Cross?

The evidence for the post-Resurrection appearances of Jesus didn't develop gradually over the years as mythology distorted memories of His life. The book of Acts is littered with extremely early affirmations of Jesus' Resurrection, while the Gospels describe numerous encounters in detail. Concluded British theologian Michael Green, *"The appearances of Jesus are as well authenticated as anything in antiquity . . . There can be no rational doubt that they occurred."*

– Are there any supporting facts that point to the Resurrection?

J.P. Moreland's circumstantial evidence added final documentation for the Resurrection. First, the disciples were in a unique position to know whether the Resurrection happened, and they went to their deaths proclaiming it was true. Nobody knowingly and willingly dies for a lie. Second, apart from the Resurrection, there is no real good reason why skeptics like Paul and James would have been converted and would have died for their faith.   Third, within weeks of the Crucifixion, thousands of Jews began abandoning key social practices that had critical sociological and religious importance for centuries. They believed they risked damnation if they were wrong. Fourth, the early sacraments of Communion and Baptism affirmed Jesus' Resurrection and deity. And fifth, the miraculous emergence of the church in the face of brutal Roman persecution *"rips a great hole in history, a hole the size and shape of Resurrection,"* as C. F. D. Moule put it.

What clinched it for Lee Strobel was this: *"A famous study by A. Sherwin-White, the great classical historian from Oxford University, meticulously examined the rate at which a legend occurred in the ancient world. His conclusion: not even two full generations was enough time for a legend to develop and wipe out a solid core of historical truth. Now consider the case of Jesus. Historically speaking, the news of His empty tomb, the eye witness accounts of his post Resurrection appearances, and the conviction that He was indeed God's unique son emerged virtually instantaneously."*

Strobel concludes, *"In light of the convincing facts I had learned during my investigation, in the face of this overwhelming avalanche of evidence in the case of Christ, the great irony is this: It would require much more faith for me to maintain my atheism than to trust in Jesus of Nazareth."*

    Strobel's book along with McDowell's and many others point to one thing:

Jesus Christ is the Son of God who came to this earth to redeem sinful man.

Conclusion

I look back at my life, growing up in a Muslim society and trying to redeem myself with my good deeds. I look back at all of the years of questioning in college and up to the aneurysm, then the period of four years after the aneurysm. Then I look back at the period of twelve years after my near-conversion without the Savior, and I can do nothing but bow my head in humility and adoration and say *Thank you*:

Thank you for choosing an Arab boy who wanted to experience your love.

Thank you for giving me the time to wonder and think and reflect.

Thank you for enabling me to believe in the Savior.

Thank you for having me receive the Holy Spirit to dwell within me.

Thank you for dying on the Cross to redeem me from my sins.

And lastly, thank you for making my heart long to love you, my brain to decipher truth from fiction, my body to carry on your mission, and my soul to accept a God that not only loves me and wants to dwell in me, but who also gave up His life for me.

Your Journey

"Therefore, as you received Christ Jesus the Lord, so walk in him."
Colossians 2:6

_____

_____

_____

_____

_____

_____

_____

_____

_____

_____

_____

_____

_____

_____

Paul's Journey Ends in Martyrdom
by James Stalker

Voyage to Italy.—The journal of the voyage has been preserved in the Acts of the Apostles and is acknowledged to be the most valuable document in existence concerning the seamanship of ancient times. It is also a precious document of Paul's life; for it shows how his character shone out in a novel situation. A ship is a kind of miniature of the world. It is a floating island, in which there are the government and the governed. But the government is, like that of states, liable to sudden social upheavals, in which the ablest man is thrown to the top. This was a voyage of extreme perils, which required the utmost presence of mind and power of winning the confidence and obedience of those on board. Before it was ended Paul was virtually both the captain of the ship and the general of the soldiers; and all on board owed to him their lives.

Arrival in Rome.—At length the dangers of the deep were left behind; and Paul found himself approaching the capital of the Roman world by the Appian Road, the great highway by which Rome was entered by travelers from the East. The bustle and noise increased as he neared the city, and the signs of Roman grandeur and renown multiplied at every step. For many years he had been looking forward to seeing Rome, but he had always thought of entering it in a very different guise from that which now he wore. He had always thought of Rome as a successful general thinks of the central stronghold of the country he is subduing, who looks eagerly forward to the day when he will direct the charge against its gates. Paul was engaged in the conquest of the world for Christ, and Rome was the final position he had hoped to carry in his Master's name. Years ago he had sent to it the famous challenge, "I am ready to preach the gospel to you that are at Rome also; for I am not ashamed of the gospel of Christ, for it is the power of God unto salvation to everyone that believeth." But now, when he found himself actually at its gates and thought of the abject condition in which he was—an old, gray-haired, broken man, a chained prisoner just escaped from shipwreck—his heart sank within him, and he felt dreadfully alone.

At the right moment, however, a little incident took place which restored him to himself: at a small town forty miles out of Rome he was met by a little band of Christian brethren, who, hearing of his approach, had come out to welcome him; and, ten miles farther on, he came upon another group, who had come out for the same purpose. Self-reliant as he was, he was exceedingly sensitive to human sympathy, and the sight of these brethren and their interest in him completely revived him. He thanked God and took courage; his old feelings came back in their wonted strength; and, when, in the company of these friends, he reached that shoulder of the Alban Hills from which the first view of the city is obtained, his heart swelled with the anticipation of victory; for he knew he carried in his breast the force which would yet lead captive that proud capital.

It was not with the step of a prisoner, but with that of a conqueror, that he passed at length beneath the city gate. His road lay along that very Sacred Way by which many a Roman general had passed in triumph to the Capitol, seated on a car of victory, followed by the prisoners and spoils of the enemy, and surrounded with the plaudits of rejoicing Rome. Paul looked little like such a hero: no car of victory carried him, he trode the causewayed road with way-worn foot; no medals or ornaments adorned his person, a chain of iron dangled from his wrist; no applauding crowds welcomed his approach, a few humble friends formed all his escort; yet never did a more truly conquering footstep fall on the pavement of Rome or a heart more confident of victory pass within her gates.

Imprisonment.—Meanwhile, however, it was not to the Capitol his steps were bent, but to a prison; and he was destined to lie in prison long, for his trial did not come on for two years. The law's delays have been proverbial in all countries and at all eras; and the law of imperial Rome was not likely to be free from this reproach during the reign of Nero, a man of such frivolity that any engagement of pleasure or freak of caprice was sufficient to make him put off the most important call of business. The imprisonment, it is true, was of the mildest description. It may have been that the officer who brought him to Rome spoke a good word for the man who had saved his life during the voyage, or the officer to whom he was handed over, and who is known in profane history as a man of justice and humanity, may have inquired into his case and formed a favorable opinion of his character; but at all events

Paul was permitted to hire a house of his own and live in it in perfect freedom, with the single exception that a soldier, who was responsible for his person, was his constant attendant.

Occupation in Prison.—This was far from the condition which such an active spirit would have coveted. He would have liked to be moving from synagogue to synagogue in the immense city, preaching in its streets and squares, and founding congregation after congregation among the masses of its population. Another man, thus arrested in a career of ceaseless movement and immured within prison walls, might have allowed his mind to stagnate in sloth and despair. But Paul behaved very differently. Availing himself of every possibility of the situation, he converted his one room into a center of far-reaching activity and beneficence. On the few square feet of space allowed him he erected a fulcrum with which he moved the world, establishing within the walls of Nero's capital a sovereignty more extensive than his own.

Even the most irksome circumstance of his lot was turned to good account. This was the soldier by whom he was watched. To a man of Paul's eager temperament and restlessness of mood this must often have been an intolerable annoyance; and, indeed, in the letters written during this imprisonment he is constantly referring to his chain, as if it were never out of his mind. But he did not suffer this irritation to blind him to the opportunity of doing good presented by the situation. Of course his attendant was changed every few hours, as one soldier relieved another upon guard. In this way there might be six or eight with him every four-and-twenty hours. They belonged to the imperial guard, the flower of the Roman army.

Paul could not sit for hours beside another man without speaking of the subject which lay nearest his heart. He spoke to these soldiers about their immortal souls and the faith of Christ. To men accustomed to the horrors of Roman warfare and the manners of Roman barracks nothing could be more striking than a life and character like his; and the result of these conversations was that many of them became changed men, and a revival spread through the barracks and penetrated into the imperial household itself. His room was sometimes crowded with these stern, bronzed faces, glad to see him at other times than those when duty required them to be there. He sympathized with them and entered into the spirit of their occupation; indeed, he was full of the spirit of the warrior himself.

We have an imperishable relic of these visits in an outburst of inspired eloquence which he dictated at this period: "Put on the whole armor of God, that ye may be able to stand against the wiles of the devil; for we wrestle not against flesh and blood, but against principalities, against powers, against the rulers of the darkness of this world, against spiritual wickedness in high places. Wherefore take unto you the whole armor of God, that ye may be able to withstand in the evil day and, having done all, to stand. Stand therefore, having your loins girt about with truth, and having on the breastplate of righteousness, and your feet shod with the preparation of the gospel of peace; above all, taking the shield of faith, wherewith ye shall be able to quench all the fiery darts of the wicked. And take the helmet of salvation and the sword of the Spirit, which is the word of God." That picture was drawn from the life, from the armor of the soldiers in his room; and perhaps these ringing sentences were first poured into the ears of his warlike auditors before they were transferred to the Epistle in which they have been preserved.

Visitors.—But he had other visitors. All who took an interest in Christianity in Rome, both Jews and Gentiles, gathered to him. Perhaps there was not a day of the two years of his imprisonment but he had such visitors. The Roman Christians learned to go to that room as to an oracle or shrine. Many a Christian teacher got his sword sharpened there; and new energy began to diffuse itself through the Christian circles of the city. Many an anxious father brought his son, many a friend his friend, hoping that a word from the apostle's lips might waken the sleeping conscience. Many a wanderer, stumbling in there by chance, came out a new man. Such an one was Onesimus, a slave from Colossae, who arrived in Rome as a runaway, but was sent back to his Christian master, Philemon, no longer as a slave, but as a brother beloved.

Still more interesting visitors came. At all periods of his life he exercised a strong fascination over young men. They were attracted by the manly soul within him, in which they found sympathy with their aspirations and inspiration for the noblest work. These youthful friends, who were scattered over the world in the work of Christ, flocked to him at Rome.

Timothy and Luke, Mark and Aristarchus, Tychicus and Epaphras, and many more came, to drink afresh at the well of his ever-springing wisdom and earnestness. And he sent them forth again, to carry messages to his churches or bring him news of their condition.

Of his spiritual children in the distance he never ceased to think. Daily he was wandering in imagination among the glens of Galatia and along the shores of Asia and Greece; every night he was praying for the Christians of Antioch and Ephesus, of Philippi and Thessalonica and Corinth. Nor were gratifying proofs awanting that they were remembering him. Now and then there would appear in his lodging a deputy from some distant church, bringing the greetings of his converts or, perhaps, a contribution to meet his temporal wants, or craving his decision on some point of doctrine or practice about which difficulty had arisen. These messengers were not sent empty away: they carried warm-hearted messages of golden words of counsel from their apostolic friend.

Some of them carried far more. When Epaphroditus, a deputy from the church at Philippi, which had sent to their dear father in Christ an offering of love, was returning home, Paul sent with him, in acknowledgment of their kindness, the Epistle to the Philippians, the most beautiful of all his letters, in which he lays bare his very heart and every sentence glows with love more tender than a woman's. When the slave Onesimus was sent back to Colossae, he received, as the branch of peace to offer to his master, the exquisite little Epistle to Philemon, a priceless monument of Christian courtesy. He carried, too, a letter addressed to the church of the town in which his master lived, the Epistle to the Colossians.

The composition of these Epistles was by far the most important part of Paul's varied prison activity; and he crowned this labor with the writing of the Epistle to the Ephesians, which is perhaps the profoundest and sublimest book in the world. The Church of Christ has derived many benefits from the imprisonment of the servants of God; the greatest book of uninspired religious genius, the Pilgrim's Progress, was written in a jail; but never did there come to the Church a greater mercy in the disguise of misfortune than when the arrest of Paul's bodily activities at Caesarea and Rome supplied him with the leisure needed to reach the depths of truth sounded in the Epistle to the Ephesians.

His Prison Writings.—It may have seemed a dark dispensation of providence to Paul himself that the course of life he had pursued so long was so completely changed; but God's thoughts are higher than man's thoughts and His ways than man's ways; and He gave Paul grace to overcome the temptations of his situation and do far more in his enforced inactivity for the welfare of the world and the permanence of his own influence than he could have done by twenty years of wandering missionary work. Sitting in his room, he gathered within the sounding cavity of his sympathetic heart the sighs and cries of thousands far away, and diffused courage and help in every direction from his own inexhaustible resources. He sank his mind deeper and deeper in solitary thought, till, smiting the rock in the dim depth to which he had descended, he caused streams to gush forth which are still gladdening the city of God.

Release from Prison.—The book of Acts suddenly breaks off with a brief summary of Paul's two years' imprisonment at Rome. Is this because there was no more to tell? When his trial came on, did it issue in his condemnation and death? Or did he get out of prison and resume his old occupations? Where Luke's lucid narrative so suddenly deserts us, tradition comes in proffering its doubtful aid. It tells us that he was acquitted on his trial and let out of prison; that he resumed his travels, visiting Spain among other places; but that before long he was arrested again and sent back to Rome, where he died a martyr's death at the cruel hands of Nero.

New Journeys.—Happily, however, we are not altogether dependent on the precarious aid of tradition. We have writings of Paul's own undoubtedly subsequent to the two years of his first imprisonment. These are what are called the Pastoral Epistles—the Epistles to Timothy and Titus. In these we see that he regained his liberty and resumed his employment of revisiting his old churches and founding new ones. His footsteps cannot, indeed, be any longer traced with certainty. We find him back at Ephesus and Troas; we find him in Crete, an island at which he touched on his voyage to Rome and in which he may then have become interested; we find him exploring new territory in the northern parts of Greece. We see him once more, like the commander of an army who sends his aides-de-camp all over the field of battle, sending out his young assistants to organize and watch over the churches.

But this was not to last long. An event had happened immediately after his release from prison which could not but influence his fate. This was the burning of Rome—an appalling disaster, the glare of which even at this distance makes the heart shudder. It was probably a mad freak of the malicious monster who then wore the imperial purple. But Nero saw fit to attribute it to the Christians, and instantly the most atrocious persecution broke out against them. Of course the fame of this soon spread over the Roman world; and it was not likely that the foremost apostle of Christianity could long escape. Every Roman governor knew that he could not do the emperor a more pleasing service than by sending to him Paul in chains.

Second Imprisonment.—It was not long, accordingly, before Paul was lying once more in prison at Rome; and it was no mild imprisonment this time, but the worst known to the law. No troops of friends now filled his room; for the Christians of Rome had been massacred or scattered, and it was dangerous for anyone to avow himself a Christian. We have a letter written from his dungeon, the last he ever wrote, the Second Epistle to Timothy, which affords us a glimpse of unspeakable pathos into the circumstances of the prisoner. He tells us that one part of his trial is already over. Not a friend stood by him as he faced the bloodthirsty tyrant who sat on the judgment-seat. But the Lord stood by him and enabled him to make the emperor and the spectators in the crowded basilica hear the sound of the gospel. The charge against him had broken down. But he had no hope of escape. Other stages of the trial had yet to come, and he knew that evidence to condemn him would either be discovered or manufactured.

The letter betrays the miseries of his dungeon. He prays Timothy to bring a cloak he had left at Troas, to defend him from the damp of the cell and the cold of the winter. He asks for his books and parchments, that he may relieve the tedium of his solitary hours with the studies he had always loved. But, above all, he beseeches Timothy to come himself; for he was longing to feel the touch of a friendly hand and see the face of a friend yet once again before he died.

Was the brave heart then conquered at last? Read the Epistle and see. How does it begin? "I also suffer these things; nevertheless I am not ashamed; for I know whom I have believed, and am persuaded that He is able to keep that which I have committed unto Him against that day." How does it end? "I am now ready to be offered, and the time of my departure is at hand. I have fought a good fight, I have finished my course, I have kept the faith. Henceforth there is laid up for me a crown of righteousness, which the Lord, the righteous Judge, shall give me at that day; and not to me only, but unto all them that love His appearing." That is not the strain of the vanquished.

His Final Trial.—There can be little doubt that he appeared again at Nero's bar, and this time the charge did not break down. In all history there is not a more startling illustration of the irony of human life than this scene of Paul at the bar of Nero. On the judgment-seat, clad in the imperial purple, sat a man who in a bad world had attained the eminence of being the very worst and meanest being in it—a man stained with every crime, the murderer of his own mother, of his wives and of his best benefactors; a man whose whole being was so steeped in every namable and unnamable vice that body and soul of him were, as someone said at the time, nothing but a compound of mud and blood; and in the prisoner's dock stood the best man the world contained, his hair whitened with labors for the good of men and the glory of God. Such was the occupant of the seat of justice, and such the man who stood in the place of the criminal.

His Death.—The trial ended, Paul was condemned and delivered over to the executioner. He was led out of the city with a crowd of the lowest rabble at his heels. The fatal spot was reached; he knelt beside the block; the headsman's axe gleamed in the sun and fell; and the head of the apostle of the world rolled down in the dust.

So sin did its uttermost and its worst. Yet how poor and empty was its triumph! The blow of the axe only smote off the lock of the prison and let the spirit go forth to its home and to its crown. The city falsely called eternal dismissed him with execration from her gates; but ten thousand times ten thousand welcomed him in the same hour at the gates of the city which is really eternal. Even on earth Paul could not die. He lives among us to-day with a life a hundredfold more influential than that which throbbed in his brain whilst the earthly form which made him visible still lingered on the earth. Wherever the feet of them who publish the glad tidings go forth beautiful upon the mountains, he walks by their side as an inspirer and a guide; in ten thousand churches every Sabbath and on a thousand thousand hearths every day his eloquent lips still teach that gospel of which he was never ashamed; and, wherever there are human souls searching for the white flower of holiness or climbing the difficult heights of self-denial, there he whose life was so pure, whose devotion to Christ was so entire, and whose pursuit of a single purpose was so unceasing, is welcomed as the best of friends.

EPILOGUE

What I Desire the Reader to Gain From This Book

My journey from Islam to Christianity is the workmanship of a new soul and a new heart, and the journey of writing about it has been soul penetrating and heart permeating. God has given me a brand new life by believing and trusting in His Son, Jesus Christ, and through the fellowship with His Holy Spirit. My conversion was the starting point of this new life. Through conversion, my principles have changed. What I held as darkness, I now call light. I am experiencing what Saint Paul expressed in 2 Corinthians 5:17, *"Therefore, if anyone is in Christ, he is a new creation. The old has passed away; behold, the new has come."*

The idea of redemption is phenomenal - that Christ came to redeem us from our sins once and for all by becoming the perfect sacrifice of atonement. Man has tried to redeem himself with different sacrifices from the beginning of time. The idea of the shedding of blood to wash away sins goes back to Cain and Abel. I never understood redemption and the power behind it until I read John Murray's book, *Redemption – Accomplished and Ap-*

plied: "Not only is Christ regarded as having died for the believer, but the believer is represented as having died in Christ and as having been raised up with Him to newness of life. This is the result of union with Christ."

Saint Paul describes this union in Romans 6:1-10:

"What shall we say, then? Shall we go on sinning so that grace may increase? By no means! We are those who have died to sin; how can we live in it any longer? Or don't you know that all of us who were baptized into Christ Jesus were baptized into his death? We were therefore buried with him through baptism into death in order that, just as Christ was raised from the dead through the glory of the Father, we too may live a new life. For if we have been united with him in a death like his, we will certainly also be united with him in a resurrection like his. For we know that our old self was crucified with him so that the body ruled by sin might be done away with, that we should no longer be slaves to sin— because anyone who has died has been set free from sin. Now if we died with Christ, we believe that we will also live with him. For we know that since Christ was raised from the dead, he cannot die again; death no longer has mastery over him. The death he died, he died to sin once for all; but the life he lives, he lives to God."

A new seed has been planted in the depths of my soul. My hope is that this seed will sprout and grow to heights insurmountable. It will grow thick roots, helping me fight sin and temptation; it will grow a sturdy trunk to lean on during storms; and it will grow high enough to peek at His Kingdom and count the days until I am with Him in glory.

The act of writing about my conversion has been as healing as a serene walk in His ardent light. As I wrote this book, I realized that every chapter could have an appeal to the readers. Perhaps, I thought, they can avoid the difficulties and drawbacks I experienced. Perhaps they can sense the trials and tribulations encountered while trying to submit to Jesus Christ as my Lord and Savior. And perhaps they can accomplish their own goals without enduring my failures.

This epilogue is by no means a section to read over in a hurry. It ought to be reflected upon and studied with the most contemplation and scrutiny. Consider one or more of these appeals to be your mission – as they are my mission. Accomplish them one at a time. They can enhance your reach for Christ if you are not yet a true believer in Him. They can also assist you in spreading His message of faith, hope, and love if you *have* come to place your trust fully in Him.

Mission One – Endure Turmoil

Despite all the pain I endured during my aneurysm - despite the hardship, the long recovery, and the permanent side effects - despite the fact that it had much to do with my divorce - despite everything. . . that aneurysm was by far the *best thing* that ever happened to me. It led me to Christ.

If you had come to me as my brain exploded at the church fire, or as I was thrashing in bed trying to come out of the belts they tied me with, or while I was learning to talk and walk, or when for days I looked at the nurse with tears in my eyes because I couldn't say "My head hurts"; and said, "Karim, trust me – what is happening is for your own good," I would have dismissed you as a fool and cursed you as a lunatic.

Appeal

When bad things take place in your life, when deep trouble visits you and turns your life upside down, be still and know that God is speaking. Don't make rash decisions, and don't come to quick judgments. Wait and see what the long-term results are. See what the big picture is. God has a plan for your life. He is in total control and has a course of action that is most wonderful and most fulfilling. Seek Him humbly in earnest prayer that He will direct your steps.

Action Verse

"Trust in the Lord with all your heart, and do not lean on your own understanding. In all your ways acknowledge him, and he will make straight your paths." Proverbs 3:5,6

Mission Two – Sanctify Life

Had my mother gone through with the abortion, some might say there would just be one less life on this planet. If you think about it, you wouldn't have read this book. None of the people I have interacted with over the years would have known me. I don't want to use the *It's a Wonderful Life* metaphor, but it does make you wonder. What if I was not born? What if George Washington was not born? Or C. S. Lewis, or George Whitefield, or J.I Packer, or St. Monica - the mother of Augustine, or Elisabeth Elliot, or John Calvin, or Martin Luther, or Charles Spurgeon, or Lee Strobel, or Fanny Crosby, or John Stott? Is that *just* one less life? What about the millions of lives they have impacted? I am not comparing myself to these giants. I am just saying that every life is precious and has the potential to reach at least one lost soul.

Life is a gift to all of us, yet many do not receive it. Every day, countless abortions take place in this country and around the world. It brings tears to my eyes because it hits on a personal level to think of all the innocent babies killed because of something we call "free choice." Why is the taking of innocent life considered free choice? You go to jail for killing someone. Why is abortion allowed? The events in Newtown, Connecticut, were beyond horrific. I cried when I found out twenty little children and six adults were slaughtered. Then I heard this statistic: forty-six children are aborted in the State of Connecticut every day, and over four thousand in the United States every day. In no way am I stating the Newtown massacre was not abominable. I am simply asking why those countless children that are slaughtered in the womb every day go ignored.

Appeal

If you know of someone who is considering abortion, or if you yourself are contemplating one, I beg you to reconsider and bring the child into this world. There are many options you can take like adoption. You don't have to take the life of the baby while in the womb. You will be blessed.

If you have already had an abortion, my heart breaks for you as I cannot imagine the pain you have to endure. The wonderful message of the Gospel is that there is forgiveness from all sin, and we can be set free and given a new beginning.

Action Verse

"For you formed my inward parts; you knitted me together in my mother's womb. I praise you, for I am fearfully and wonderfully made. Wonderful are your works, my soul knows it very well." Psalm 139:13,14

Mission Three – Ask Questions

I could have saved myself two serious paddlings and the fear of my father rejecting my question had it not been known. Was it worth it? You bet. That question—*Did God make man, or did man make God?*—led me to explore religion on a deep level that would ultimately lead me to Christ. We are often afraid of provocative thoughts, and thus deny them exposure to the light.

Appeal

Be TRANSPARENT. Have the courage to ask the tough questions regardless of the consequences. You never know the impact the answer, or the question itself, can have on your life.

Action Verse

"Now to him who is able to do far more abundantly than all that we ask or think, according to the power at work within us, to him be glory in the church and in Christ Jesus throughout all generations, forever and ever. Amen." Ephesians 3:20,21

Mission Four – Embrace Change

Abraham left his homeland upon God's bare command. Jacob waited seven years to have Rachel. Joseph was sold into slavery and would end up saving his family. Moses led the Israelites towards the Promised Land despite feeling his own inadequacies. Joshua conquered the Land of Canaan despite the defeat at the Battle of Ai, and Daniel withstood a den of lions.

Sometimes we are faced with drastic, life-altering decisions. Don't forget: it is all a part of God's plan. Big decisions can scare us, and all we have to do is trust in the Lord.

Appeal

If the status quo is opposing to God's Will for your life, take the proper steps and *fear not*. There is a reason the phrase *fear not* is mentioned over three hundred times in the Bible. That reason is that the presence, promise, and power of the Lord remove all cause of fear.

Action Verse

"For God gave us a spirit not of fear but of power and love and self-control." 2 Timothy 1:7

Mission Five – Seize Time

When things seem obvious. When they are screaming at us from all different directions. When they rage in our hearts and minds - we ought to take action. We ought to be courageous, and let the tiny distractions fall by the wayside. We are responsible if we delay action or never take it. It took me four years to make a half of a step towards His Salvation, then it would take me twelve more years to finally surrender to his will.

Carpe Diem - Seize the Day.

Appeal

What are you waiting for? A beam of light to shine from Heaven letting you know that your time has arrived? A major event in your life to signal you to move forward? Sometimes we just have to pray to God and dive in. Believing in the Son will only lead to accomplishing the will of God in our life.

Action Verse

"And working together with Him, we also urge you not to receive the grace of God in vain— for He says, 'At the acceptable time I listened to you, and on the day of salvation I helped you.' Behold, now is 'the acceptable time,' behold, now is 'the day of salvation.'" 2 Corinthians 6:1, 2

Mission Six – Welcome Death

When I lost my father, I thought my life was over. A week later, the sky turned blue and birds started chirping again. And while life on earth is precious, life with the Heavenly Father is much more to be treasured. He longs for us to live on this planet and accomplish His will. At the same time, we should long to be with Him.

Appeal

Losing a loved one does not have to be the end. Celebrate those who have gone to be with the Lord. Comfort their family by reminding them that their loved one is in the hands of God, and that He will do what is right.

Action Verse

"When the perishable puts on the imperishable, and the mortal puts on immortality, then shall come to pass the saying that is written: 'Death is swallowed up in victory.' 'O death, where is your victory? O death, where is your sting?' The sting of death is sin, and the power of sin is the law. But

thanks be to God, who gives us the victory through our Lord Jesus Christ."
1 Corinthians 15:54-57

Mission Seven – Rejoice in Adversity

The economic decline rendered me homeless for over a year, a period of my life I wish to never repeat. Albeit, the lessons I learned were extremely valuable. Not every bad thing turns out to be good, but we just have to trust in the Lord and submit.

Appeal

Has the economy taken a toll on your job, your family, and your life? Hang in there and trust the Lord. It may be the right time to learn obedience to God. He will not forsake you. This planet is filled with sin and its aftermath. The only way to rise above sin is through Jesus Christ.

Action Verse

"And my God will supply every need of yours according to his riches in glory in Christ Jesus." Philippians 4:19

Mission Eight – Treasure a Teacher

I cannot say enough about how important it is to have a mentor guiding you and teaching you about the Kingdom of God. Rev. Frank Barker has become more than a father figure in my life. What this man has done for my faith-life is inconceivable, yet he presses on and continues teaching me to grow in Christ.

Appeal

ind someone you trust and who has solid knowledge of the
ures. Ask them to guide you. Finding the time can be tough,
nsider this to be the number one priority and arrange other
ments around it. Perhaps it is time for you to become a

mentor to another. Prayerfully, the Lord would have you guide someone in the path of righteousness for His name's sake.

Action Verse

"Be imitators of me, as I am of Christ." 1 Corinthians 11:1

Mission Nine – Affirm Freedom

While my citizenship in this country means the world to me, I aspire to live in citizenship in Christ. Freedom in Christ has no limits – man-granted freedom has a multitude of limits.

Appeal

Exercise your freedom in Christ regardless of where you live; it is much more satisfying than man-made freedom. The disciples gave up their lives for that freedom.

Action Verse

"I have been crucified with Christ. It is no longer I who live, but Christ who lives in me. And the life I now live in the flesh I live by faith in the Son of God, who loved me and gave himself for me." Galatians 2:20

Mission Ten – Positive Proof

There is much evidence that Christianity is the only way to God. To live eternally with the Father you must repent and believe in Jesus Christ dying for your sins, then you are forgiven: past – present – and future. From prophecies of the Old Testament, to evidence from history surrounding the life of Jesus, to the disciples dying for the truth, to my aneurysm on a personal level, there is a mountain of evidence that compelled me to surrender to Him. Believe that the Lord is the way, the truth, the life, and you will be saved.

Appeal

If you died right now, would you end up in Heaven? If your answer takes longer than a millisecond, you need to renew your covenant with God, through His Son Jesus Christ. This prayer may be a guide to you as you seek to express your heart to Him: "Lord Jesus, I come to you a sinner with countless faults and limitations. I am sorry. I repent and ask for your forgiveness. I believe you died on the Cross for my sins to save me. I come to you a humble and wretched human asking you to take control of my life. Help me live and surrender my will to yours. I love you and thank you for offering to me the gift of eternal life. In Jesus name, Amen."

If you sincerely prayed to the Lord in this way, you have taken your first step towards becoming a Christian. Seek and participate in a solid church where the Word of God is taken seriously. Read the Word daily, and commune in fellowship with other believers. The love of God will encompass you and guide you as you live for Christ and in Christ. There is nothing you can do to cause God to love you any less. God loves you unconditionally.

Action Verse

"'The word is near you, in your mouth and in your heart,' that is, the word of faith we proclaim: because, if you confess with your mouth that Jesus is Lord and believe in your heart that God raised him from the dead, you will be saved. For 'everyone who calls on the name of the Lord will be saved.'"
Romans 10:8, 9, 13

One Final Word

This question is on the minds of many people: How can we reach out to Muslims, Buddhists, Hindus, Jews, or anyone with a different faith?

Coming to Christianity from Islam, and considering I was one of the lost, I have the deepest and most sincere desire to share my answer. And while there are many ways to evangelize, I will tell you what worked for me:

There is no other religion that is based 100 percent on love. God came in the flesh for one reason: love. He loves us and desires to save us from our sinful nature. That is it. Simple—yet intricate; free—yet costly; a gift—yet many refuse it.

The Bible is very clear on love being the antidote for the fear of God:

"There is no fear in love, but perfect love casts out fear. For fear has to do with punishment, and whoever fears has not been perfected in love." 1 John 4:18.

This is why I was so infatuated with this love, because it had the power to suppress the fear I was raised on. When you replace fear with love, a whole new world flourishes—a world with no boundaries, a world with immense power, a world with eternal life looming. A different kind of fear is still required:

"Now when all the people saw the thunder and the flashes of lightning and the sound of the trumpet and the mountain smoking, the people were afraid and trembled, and they stood far off and said to Moses, 'You speak to us, and we will listen; but do not let God speak to us, lest we die.' Moses said to the people, 'Do not fear, for God has come to test you, that the fear of him may be before you, that you may not sin.' The people stood far off, while Moses drew near to the thick darkness where God was." Exodus 20:18-21

Moses explained to the Israelites two kinds of fear. The first is being afraid of God as the scary being who is going to bring wrath onto them, the fear they were not supposed to have. The second is fearing the God who has a heart full of love and mercy. Christians are supposed to fear the latter God. We are to fear the God who loves us, not the God who is going to destroy us - A big difference.

This love is what appealed to me and tugged on the strings of my heart to embrace Christ. It is what turned me away from fearing God to loving Him, from weighing the good versus the bad to throwing away the scale, and from guilt over sin to atonement. I dream of one day considering Christ like the Apostle Paul did, as relayed in Adolphe Monod's *Saint Paul*: *"Christ has become both the seed and the fruit, the beginning and the end, the alpha and the omega of his new life."*

The love of God is best described in 1 Corinthians 13:4-7: *"Love is patient, love is kind. It does not envy, it does not boast, it is not proud. It does not dishonor others, it is not self-seeking, it is not easily angered, it keeps no record of wrongs. Love does not delight in evil but rejoices with the truth. It always protects, always trusts, always hopes, always perseveres."*

The passage written by the Apostle Paul and recited at most weddings describes a love humans fail trying to fulfill. It is only through washing ourselves daily with the blood of the Lamb that we can even fathom such love.

This love has the power of explaining the Trinity to my humble brain. It says in 1 John 4:8, *"God is love."* For love to be present, there has to be a lover and a beloved. So as God is love, Christ is the lover, and as the Holy Spirit dwells in us, we are the beloved. I struggled with the Trinity for years before I came to this illumination, full of light and grace.

My understanding of His grace grows day by day, and my surrender to His will improves day by day. His overflowing love and amazing grace will always broaden the brinks of my being. I am still a sinful man in need of the blood of the Lamb. Paul's humility and surrender to the will of God enabled him to write phenomenal letters that continue to touch people's lives. My hope is this book will touch your life, and make you trace your own journey to our Lord and to Our Savior. May the iridescence of God's favor broaden the brinks of *your* being.

May your life abound in His love, mercy, and grace. May your faith be as strong as Saint Paul's, your hope as lofty as the Heavenly gates, and your love as alluring as the words from 1 Corinthians 13 written on your heart.

The Love I Live - The Life I Love
by Karim Shamsi-Basha

The Road to Damascus a long pilgrimage
Difficult and full of darkness and plight
Tarsus' Saul filled with hate and rage
Pushed ahead with power and might

Arrest Christ's followers his mission
His ultimate goal in life sincere
End the Way and fill the prison
With faithful in sorrow and tear

His eyes blinded his soul clipped
By a light strong with Godly might
His power gone his clout stripped
With God's potent radiance bright

Three days of silence and fasting
Filled with Jesus whispering love
Three days of agony and sting
Full of Christ's peaceful dove

It is through calamities God speaks
Making Saint Paul surrender his vision
Only to visualize God's high peaks
To be his accoutrement and provision

Salvation is his to covet and live
Endless as the waves of the sea
Graces of God to wash and give
Limitless white to our sad plea

Redemption he shares and boasts
The entire world at his command
Millions follow from coast to coast
Millions are saved by his hand

He preached Christ so we can live
Through His pain, agony, and death
His love is ours to take and give
"It is finished" our daily breath

The life I live is never the same
As I journey across the famous road
And trace the steps Saint Paul took
As he kicked against the goad

I am redeemed my debt is gone
Washed by the blood of the Lamb
His grace mercy and love abound
His forgiveness and peace I am

The love I love the life I live
He lost His to give me mine
The love I live the life I love
He sacrificed His so I can shine

The Street Called Straight

CPSIA information can be obtained at www.ICGtesting.com
Printed in the USA
LVOW12s1536301113

363232LV00043B/1493/P